TOWARD A LIBERTARIAN SOCIETY

The Mises Institute dedicates this volume to all of its generous donors and wishes to thank these Patrons, in particular:

top dog™

~

Anonymous, Michael G. Keller, DO

~

Anonymous (3), Wesley and Terri Alexander,
Harvey Allison, Thomas Balmer, Steven R. Berger,
Bob and Rita Bost, Mary E. Braum, Jon Carnes,
Wayne Chapeskie, Andrew S. Cofrin, Mike Fox,
Kevin R. Griffin, Jeffrey Harding, Dr. Ronald J. Legere II,
Robert A. Moore, Gregory and Joy Morin,
Nelson and Mary Nash, Mr. and Mrs. William C. Newton,
Paul F. Peppard, Rafael A. Perez-Mera, MD,
Daniel J. Rozeboom, Chris Rufer, William P. Sarubbi,
Donald E. Siemers, Henri Etel Skinner,
Hubert John Strecker, John Tubridy, Joseph Vierra,
Dr. Thomas L. Wenck, Brian Wilton, Tom Winn,
Mr. and Mrs. Walter Woodul III,
Guillermo M. Yeatts

Toward a Libertarian Society

Walter Block

MisesInstitute

Mises Institute
518 West Magnolia Avenue
Auburn, Alabama 36832
mises.org

ISBN: 978-1-61016-595-2 (paperback)
ISBN: 978-1-61016-631-7 (large print edition)
eISBN: 978-1-61016-629-4 (digital)

To the Memory of a Great Man,
Murray N. Rothbard

CONTENTS

Preface

What sticks out at me is that libertarianism is a three-legged stool. It consists of foreign policy, economic policy, and policy concerning personal liberties. Wait. No. That is not quite right. Yes, libertarianism does indeed consist of these three "legs" but so does every other political philosophy — Marxism, Conservatism, Left Liberalism, Progressivism, communism, Nazism, feminism — without exception. That is, *every* political philosophy, if it is to be a complete one, must address these three issues, wrestle with them, come to grips with them.

The topics I address in this book consist of a quintessentially *libertarian* answer to these challenges. And, if this material is to be consistent with that philosophy, it must adhere, strictly, to the two elements, the only two elements, of libertarianism: the non-aggression principle and private property rights based upon homesteading.

Does this book succeed in accomplishing that task? That is for others to determine. As for me, all I can say is that certainly I intend that it do so. For example, in the realm of foreign policy, the non-aggression principle would imply a policy of strict non-interventionism. This is *not* isolationism. The latter means that the U.S. pulls up its drawbridges, so to speak, and Americans have nothing to do with anyone in the rest of the world. That is not at all what the non-aggression principle requires. Citizens of our country should be free to visit, trade with, buy from, sell to, invest in, and allow investments from, people from all corners of the globe. It merely implies that the U.S. withdraw its hundreds of military bases from scores of other countries. Is this pacifism? Of course not. The proper role for the government of the U.S., to the extent that it has any proper role at all, is to engage in defense, not offense. Every basketball fan knows the difference. It is when the *other* team has the ball that they yell "Defense!" It is too bad that the average American cannot be relied upon to make this distinction consistently. What would a proper foreign policy require? Something of the sort of a very powerful Coast Guard, ready to kick the butt of anyone who would dare attack us (and shorn of its responsibilities to interdict illegal drugs, etc.).

This is why, in section I of this book, dedicated to foreign policy, I have attempted, in my own weird way, to make the case that the U.S. is at present, not a country that implements a libertarian stance, but rather one of imperialism. It swaggers its way around the planet, launching drones at people, drowning people, and using other ways to kill people, virtually none of them who have ever attacked America. And in the cases they have done so, as Ron Paul correctly insists, it was due to blowback. They are over here, he avers, because we were over there first. The solution of course is to adopt the policy laid out by George Washington and Thomas Jefferson, no "entangling alliances" and of John Quincy Adams, not going abroad in search of monsters to destroy. MYOB, mind your own business, is a far better policy than anything employed by the U.S. for most of its history. Emulating the foreign policy of Switzerland might be a good beginning.

In section II of this book, devoted to economic liberties, I try to make the case that a free enterprise system is self-sustaining, maximizes wealth, and can do better, far better, without any "help" from the state. "I'm from the government and I'm here to help you" would be the diametric opposite of the viewpoint offered here. For the so-called public sector is based upon initiatory violence, at least insofar as its compulsory taxation is concerned. And in the Rothbardian analysis, its triangular intervention, forbidding or compelling commercial interaction on the part of the residents of the country, hurts, does not help, economic well-being. My favorite chapter title in the microeconomics section is: "Want To Help the Poor and Oppressed? Encourage Laissez-faire Capitalism, You Bleeding-heart Liberal, You." Come to think of it, this applies as well to bleeding heart so-called libertarians. And this applies, in spades, to the macroeconomic sphere. Say what you will about microeconomic interventionism, it is by its very nature somewhat limited in scope. Not so the macroeconomic sphere, where the statists can do far more harm, in that their policies have an impact on every corner of the economy. It is important, too, to make the case for free market environmentalism, which is far from a contradiction in terms, no matter how our friends on the left wish it were. No, in the environmental field also, private property rights, the profit and loss system, are the last best hope for mankind, and the animal kingdom, too. As a graduate student of Gary Becker's at Columbia University, I have a great interest in labor economics, and the proportion of chapters on this topic bears this out. Unions, minimum wages, violation of "scabs" rights are all part and parcel of an Austro-libertarian analysis of this sector of the economy. I write at a time when there is a push to increase the severity of the minimum wage law. I hope that the chapters in this section of the book will play some role in heading off this evil initiative.

Section III of the book focuses on personal liberties. Libertarians need make no apologies in terms of their analysis of feminism, drug legalization, charity, or health care. Again and again, the libertarian policies, based on personal rights, are both more effective and in greater congruence with morality.

So much for the libertarian outlook on the three legs of the three-legged stool of political economy. What about libertarian theory itself? This is the subject of the concluding section IV of the book. Here, I attempt to set up the basic premises and apply them to secession, punishment theory, and politics.

I hope this book causes you to think, and question how society can function successfully without a monolithic state riding roughshod over us. It would give me great pleasure if this helped in some small way to promote our beloved philosophy, libertarianism.

Introduction

In his talk entitled "Emulate Ron Paul" delivered to the Alabama state convention of Young Americans for Liberty in Auburn, Alabama on April 6, 2013, Lew Rockwell mentioned five points. The first of them, the most important one in my view, was: "The subject of war cannot, and should not, be avoided." In this regard Lew went on to say:

> First and foremost, Ron is a critic of the warfare state. The war in Iraq, which was still a live issue when Ron first ran for the Republican nomination, had been sold to the public on the basis of lies that were transparent and insulting even by the US government's standards. The devastation — in terms of deaths, maimings, displacement, and sheer destruction — appalled every decent human being.
>
> Yes, the Department of Education is an outrage, but it is nothing next to the horrifying images of what happened to the men, women, and children of Iraq. If he wasn't going to denounce such a clear moral evil, Ron thought, what was the point of being in public life at all?
>
> Still, this is the issue strategists would have had him avoid. Just talk about the budget, talk about the greatness of America, talk about whatever everyone else was talking about, and you'll be fine. And, they neglected to add, forgotten.

15

But had Ron shied away from this issue, there would have been no Ron Paul Revolution. It was his courageous refusal to back down from certain unspeakable truths about the American role in the world that caused Americans, and especially students, to sit up and take notice.

While still in his thirties, Murray Rothbard wrote privately that he was beginning to view war as "*the* key to the whole libertarian business." Here is another way Ron Paul has been faithful to the Rothbardian tradition. Time after time, in interviews and public appearances, Ron has brought the questions posed to him back to the central issues of war and foreign policy.

Worried about the budget? You can't run an empire on the cheap. Concerned about TSA groping, or government eavesdropping, or cameras trained on you? These are the inevitable policies of a hegemon. In case after case, Ron pointed to the connection between an imperial policy abroad and abuses and outrages at home.

Inspired by Ron, libertarians began to challenge conservatives by reminding them that war, after all, is the ultimate government program. War has it all: propaganda, censorship, spying, crony contracts, money printing, skyrocketing spending, debt creation, central planning, hubris — everything we associate with the worst interventions into the economy.

I have already contributed my love letter to Ron Paul in my 2012 book *Yes to Ron Paul and Liberty*; I mention this only to explain the organization of the present book. It has five sections: I. Foreign Policy, II. Economics, and III. Personal Liberties, and IV. Libertarian Theory. Of course, the five are interconnected. But, if I had to single one out, and I did, I would choose as first and foremost as did Rockwell, and Rothbard, foreign policy. "War is the health of the state," said Randolph Bourne, and no words ever said are truer than those. War mongering has implications for economic policy; it is not for nothing that the government engages in debauchment of the currency: it helps them raise more funds than would otherwise be possible for their favorite pastime: throwing their weight around the world. It has implications for personal liberties, too. In no small part is the mischievous war on drugs a handmaiden of imperialism. I place the economics section second, since I tend to see the world more through those eye glasses than any other. The third section of the book focuses on personal liberties, surely an all important subject for all libertarians. The fourth section is about the medical issues that are needful of thought. The final section concerns the backbone of libertarian thought, its theories and core.

I thank Lew Rockwell for inviting me to put together a series of columns I wrote for LewRockwell.com over the years. I thank Stephan Kinsella and William Barnett II for their permission to include in this book essays I have co-authored with them, respectively.

Ron Paul, and Lew Rockwell for that matter, are hardly the only ones who have "been faithful to the Rothbardian tradition." Murray, my friend for many years, my mentor, my teacher, my inspiration, has motivated an entire generation of libertarians, and Austrian economists, to promote the glorious Austro-libertarian philosophy. This book is in a small way devoted to that goal. This book is dedicated to the memory of that great man, Murray N. Rothbard.

Walter Block
New Orleans, 2014

1.

Foreign Policy

CHAPTER 1

Libertarian Warmongers: A Contradiction in Terms*

The argument used by most warmongers in the present day comes down to the claim that if we don't kick Saddam's butt first, he will do just that to us, first. Sometimes this is stated more formally along the following lines: It would be a dereliction of duty for the U.S. government not to invade Iraq, since if we do not, that country will unleash its weapons of mass destruction at us.

There are several problems with this way of viewing the world.

First of all, we have already "kicked Saddam's butt" in the first Iraqi war, under Bush the Elder. We continue to do so with our "no fly zone" policy, and our interference with that country's trade. Saddam need not argue that the U.S. might attack him; America has already done so, and threatens to do so once again.

Second, throughout all of history there has never been a dictatorial aggressor, a mass murderer, who could not have agreed with this preemptive strike sentiment, and enthusiastically so. Consider Stalin as an example. Is there any doubt he could not have resorted to this sort of defense with regard to Hitler? And the reverse, of course, is equally true. Each of these "worthies" could argue that the other might attack him, and therefore he would be justified in invading the other, first.

---

*January 6, 2003.

Next, consider Attila the Hun's incursion against his neighboring tribes. Even though, we may posit, they did not threaten him, still, they were capable in principle of doing physical harm to him. Could Attila not have subscribed to the notion that since these other peoples *might* harm him, he was justified in a preemptive strike? To ask this is to answer it.

Let us move from an international to a local scenario, to see how this sort of thinking might play out. Suppose there are two men walking toward each other on the street. All of a sudden, without any provocation from the latter, A hauls off and punches B in the nose. When questioned about his behavior, A replies, "Well, B might have molested me first. The violence I employed was thus justified as a purely defensive measure." Even Jack the Ripper could have hidden behind such a "defense." After all, those women he murdered might conceivably have done him a physical harm. At least it does not constitute a logical contradiction to suppose so.

This sort of thinking, it should be obvious, is a recipe for disaster. It is an utter conflation of offense and defense. If the libertarian notion of non-aggression against non-aggressors is to make any sense at all, then surely there must be a distinction between the two concepts. If we cannot even in principle distinguish between offense and defense, our political philosophy is incoherent.

But of course we can. In order for defensive violence to be justified, the person against whom we are acting must have at least threatened us; even more clearly, he must be in the early stages of launching an attack upon us.

If he is doing none of these things, then to launch aggression against him is unjustified, at least based on the libertarian code.

It cannot be denied that Saddam had previously utilized aggression against Kuwait. But what has that to do with the U.S.? Where is it written that America should be the world's policeman? And if it is justified for the U.S. to take on this role of protector of the known universe, this would also apply to other countries.

But that is the last thing that we as libertarians should want, for this is a recipe for almost total disaster. For the libertarian anarchist, government is always and ever an affront. Even for the libertarian minarchist, this description applies to the state when it exceeds its proper and very limited bounds. Given that government is a catastrophe always and ever just waiting to explode, the last thing we want is for them to mix it up with each other. If we have to have institutions that are exercises in initiatory violence, and, it appears, we must, then at least let us all bend our efforts to keep them away from each other. They are like scorpions, and we don't want to put two or more of them in a bottle, and then shake that bottle up, especially if the rest of us have to live in that bottle, too.

The proper role for the state, according to even the limited government libertarian, is for this institution to protect the rights only of its citizens. Invading Iraq to punish it for its rights violations in Kuwait is to violate the first of these strictures. In this philosophy, further, the government can only protect its citizens when they are located within its own territory. For example, if a Canadian citizen visits Japan, and his rights are violated there, then it is the Japanese government, not the Canadian, which must put matters right. If Canada attempted to do so, there would be overlapping sovereignties: both countries would claim to be sovereign in a given geographical area. Canada should limit its protection of its tourists abroad to at most telling them that they travel at their own risk. But when any given country attempts to police the world, this is precisely the result: overlapping sovereignties, a recipe for disaster.

These remarks will appear to non-libertarians as drivel, or as misbegotten, or as hopelessly misleading. But how will they appear to libertarians, particularly those who advocate U.S. adventurism all around the world? This is a nonsense question, insofar as those who favor U.S. imperialism cannot properly be considered libertarians. They may favor the elimination of rent control, tariffs, minimum wages, subsidies to business, welfare and all other such violations in the economic sphere; they may argue for rescinding laws which prohibit victimless crimes such as prostitution, pornography, gambling, using addictive drugs, etc. But unless and until they favor a strictly non-interventionist foreign policy, one limited to self-defense, they cannot be considered libertarians.

CHAPTER 2

Bloodthirsty "Libertarians": Why Warmongers Can't Be Pro-Liberty*

The libertarian non-aggression axiom is the essence of libertarianism. Take away this axiom, and libertarianism might as well be libraryism, or vegetarianism. Thus, if a person is to be a libertarian, he *must*, he absolutely *must*, in my opinion, be able to distinguish aggression from defense.

Here's a joke. Do you know the difference between a bathroom and a living room? No? Well, don't come to my house. In this spirit I ask, do you know the difference between offense and defense? Between aggression and defense against aggression? No? Well, then, don't call yourself a libertarian.

I can't read anyone out of the libertarian movement. No one appointed me guardian of this honorific. I am just giving my humble opinion. In like manner, if you couldn't tell the difference between a hammer and a chisel, I wouldn't consider you a carpenter. If you couldn't distinguish between a brush and paint, I wouldn't consider you a painter. In much the same way, if you can't tell offense and defense apart, that is, if you believe in preemptive strikes against those who are not attacking you, then I can't consider you a libertarian even if you favor free enterprise and oppose criminalizing voluntary adult conduct.

There are areas in which well meaning and knowledgeable libertarians disagree: minarchism vs. anarchism; immigration; abortion; inalienability;

---

*January 11, 2003.

punishment theory. Although I have strong views on all of these, I recognize libertarian arguments on the other side. But not on this issue.

You don't have to wait until I actually punch you in the nose to take violent action against me. You don't even have to wait until my fist is within a yard of you, moving in your direction. However, if you haul off and punch *me* in the nose in a preemptive strike, on the grounds that I *might* punch you in the future, then you are an aggressor.

Suppose you were a Martian, looking down upon the earth, trying to figure out which earth nations were aggressors, and which were not (i.e., were defenders). You have particularly good eyesight. So much so, that you can see actual uniforms, flags, etc. You notice that one country, call it Ruritania, has soldiers on the territory of scores of other nations, and sailors in every ocean known to man.

You discern that another country, Moldavia, has its armed forces in but just a few countries other than itself. And that's it. No other country has foreign military bases. What do you conclude? If you are a rational Martian, you deduce that Ruritania to a great degree, and Moldavia to a lesser one, are aggressor nations.

Suppose that your Martian eyesight also allows you to read earthling history books. There you learn that Ruritania fought worldwide wars twice in the last century, and has physically invaded, oh, give or take, about 100 countries during that time. Further, that Ruritania was the only nation in the entire history of the world to have used an atom bomb on people; worse, that they used this satanic device on *civilians*, not even soldiers; that they did so to get an unconditional surrender (Ruritania refused to promise to allow the emperor of the defeated nation to remain on his throne) from a country they pushed and hounded into war in the first place.

Who would you think was the rogue nation? Who would you think was a danger to the entire world? Who would you think was an aggressor?

But wait. Let's try to reconcile legalizing victimless crimes with not being able to tell the difference between initiation of violence and defense against it. Why legalize heroin, or alcohol for that matter? Surely it is true that those who use these substances are more likely to commit crimes than those who do not.

If you really believe in preemptive strikes against people not involved in a "clear and present danger," then how can you justify legalization? Surely, to be logically consistent, you would have to throw in jail all those who use addictive drugs.

Nor need we stop there. It just so happens that young males commit proportionately far more crimes of violence than any other cohort of the population. Under the preemptive strike philosophy, we would be justified in putting them all in jail, say, when they turn 15, and letting them out when they reach 25. Thus, if the preemptive strikers were logically coherent, not only could he not be a libertarian in foreign policy, he could not favor this philosophy even in this area.

CHAPTER 3

Thirteenth Floors*

I t is well known that 13 is an unlucky number. If you don't believe me, look it up! It is for this reason that in the U.S. and a few other civilized countries, there are no thirteenth floors in high rise buildings. We go directly from the twelfth floor to the fourteenth. And this is all to the good. It is for this reason that we, and, as I say, a mere handful of other civilized countries, have not been plagued with the bad luck visited on the rest of the world.

So far, however, America has done nothing, nothing I tell you, to alleviate this problem on a worldwide basis. But what does it profit a nation such as ours, which has achieved a preeminent position, spiritually, morally, economically, and, most important, militarily, if we will not share our civilizing influences with our beknighted neighbors?

Thus, here is the plan.

First, we put our own house in order; we pass a constitutional amendment, by executive decree, banning all thirteenth floors from the home of the brave and the land of the free; yes, whiners will object that this is unconstitutional, but surely we must reject this "argument" given the present emergency. In any case, that ancient and now irrelevant document called

---

*April 5, 2004.

for Congress to declare war; an entire series of "police actions" has rendered that a dead letter. If for war, then why not for thirteenth floors, ask I.

Second, we announce to the entire globe that henceforth no new buildings are to be erected anywhere on earth with thirteenth floors in them. If they ignore this non-negotiable demand, we will bomb only those buildings, with our sophisticated pin point accurate weapons of mass destruction, leaving all else undisturbed.

Third, we give everyone one year to convert their present housing to the U.S. model. We are nothing if not generous! In this vein, we leave it entirely up to them whether they merely want to renumber their floors to be compatible with the American practice, or, if they wish, to physically eliminate these vile floors, so as to accomplish the same ends. However, if they refuse to abide by this modest proposal, we will have no choice but to invade their countries, all of them, and make these changes ourselves.

It is time, it is long past time, that the rest of the world be brought into conformity with U.S. architectural practices. Because of them, we have been lucky: among the jewels in our crown are multiculturalism, feminism, the U.S. Constitution, the drug war, and queer studies.

Of late, however, it must be admitted, a certain amount of bad luck has come our way. Under this rubric must be counted the murder of the innocents at Ruby Ridge, the Waco massacre, and the 9/11 tragedy. But these have come about not because of any flaws in the American Experiment (applause at this point, please), but, rather, due to the failure of many other countries (they know who they are!) to, wait for it, eliminate their thirteenth floors. This constitutes an external diseconomy. As is well known to all neoclassical economists, market failures of this sort justify government action to alleviate them. Since the U.S. is now the world government, it is fully in keeping with our global obligations to uphold property rights in this manner.

Yes, yes, there are some ignoramuses, mainly Austrian economists, who reject this notion of negative externalities constituting market failure, and justifying governmental ameliorating action of the sort now being proposed. But they are few and far between, and thus, incorrect. There are also, it cannot be denied, traitors in our midst, who oppose U.S. foreign military interventionism. They are silly wusses. They do not realize just how unlucky are thirteenth floors, nor that, unless we rid ourselves of this scourge, the world will never be safe for Democracy.

Please note: this is a parody.

CHAPTER 4

Let's Go Commie, Well, Kerry*

D ear Mr. Kerry: For God's sake, we've got to get rid of that impe-
rialist war-mongering socialist fascist George Bush! You've got
to go the Gene McCarthy route. It's not too late. You can jettison
that baloney about getting the U.N. involved in the carnage. No!
The only way to get elected is to pull out now, and offer reparations for the
many sins of the U.S. government (previous administration, of course). So
far, at least as president, you haven't murdered a single solitary innocent
person. Let's try to keep it that way, shall we?

Enough with this me too-ism on Iraq. The Republicans can out-war
you any day. In that direction lies the fate of Gore, Humphrey, ... Don't you
want to win? Surely, you'd like to be president, wouldn't you? Wasn't that
the whole purpose of the primaries?

Now look. Full disclosure here. I'm a libertarian. I don't like your socialism any more than I like the Bush variety. In some ways, you're even
worse, beholden as you are to some of the worst elements in the domestic
polity: teachers, unionists, welfare queens, and Hollywood, as well as organized, victimological gays, women, blacks, Jews, Hispanics, etc. But I'm
willing to overlook all that. Anything, to see that the monster Bush gets his
just desserts come election time.

---

*July 8, 2004.

I don't much care if you wreck health care by imposing that wicked and inefficient Canadian system. It bothers me very little that you'll pack the Supreme Court with judges who will take affirmative action to new and presently unimaginable depths. I fully expect that the first step in your administration will be to force helmets on bicyclists; heck, even on joggers, or people who merely go out for a walk. You can even make Barbra Streisand your Secretary of Labor and Jane Fonda your Secretary of Commerce. I'm willing to tolerate all of this and more, if only you stop this mass murder of innocents in the Middle East, and of course the potential for it everywhere else.

So here's the deal. I will root for you in the coming election if you just borrow a leaf from Washington's "Farewell Address" or read, digest, and act upon that of John Quincy Adams speaking on the Fourth of July, 1821, who stated:

> Wherever the standard of freedom and independence has been unfurled, there will [America's] heart, her benedictions, and her prayers be. But she goes not abroad in search of monsters to destroy. She is the well-wisher to the freedom and independence of all. She is the champion and vindicator only of her own. ... She well knows that, by once enlisting under other banners than her own, were they even the banners of foreign independence, she would involve herself, beyond the power of extrication, in all the wars of interest and intrigue, of individual avarice, envy and ambition, which assume the color and usurp the standard of freedom. The fundamental maxims of her policy would insensibly change from liberty to force. The frontlets upon her brows would no longer beam with the ineffable splendor of freedom and independence; but in its stead would soon be substituted an imperial diadem, flashing in false and tarnished luster the murky radiance of dominion and power. She might become the dictatress of the world; she would no longer be the ruler of her own spirit.

I can't vote for you; sorry. I never vote; it just encourages them. (Ok, when I was young and foolish, I voted for Barry in 1964; but that was the last time! Honest!) In any case, if I voted, I'd have to vote for Michael Badnarik, the candidate for the Libertarian Party. It's an aesthetic thing, you wouldn't understand. But I will root for you, at least *vis-à-vis* that monster, Bush, if you make a 180 degree turn in your foreign policy. Think Switzerland. The

U.S. as a sort of gigantic Switzerland, which offends no one, which minds its own business.

So here's what you've got to do. Pull out all our troops from everywhere. Now! (Ok, ok, wait until you are elected.) If you learn we've got some soldiers on the moon or Mars, this goes for them as well. No more foreign military bases. Ok, ok, you can have as many foreign military bases as Switzerland has. Tell you what I'll do: I won't even insist you disband all our consulates abroad. This goes to show you just how moderate a libertarian like me can be. And they call me an extremist! Faugh! I hope and trust you appreciate my forbearance on this matter.

Then, socialism, glorious socialism. Onward and upward! Nationalize the steel mills. They are just a bunch of slobs who for far too long now have been hiding behind tariff protections. Take over the auto industry! Surely, the people who run the motor vehicle bureau offices and the post office can make better cars than Toyota? Raise the minimum wage to, oh, about $100 per hour. The present levels are unconscionable for a "progressive" such as yourself. Go green: prohibit people from exhaling; it ruins the environment. The only reason full-bore socialism didn't work in the U.S.S.R. is because they didn't have the right leaders. But I have every confidence in you (and Jane and Barbra). Just stop the mass murder, ok? (Said in the tone of voice employed by the guidance counselor in South Park.)

CHAPTER 5

Kill 'Em All: Let's All Turn Libertarian Warmonger[*]

S ave some liberal wieners and a few ungrateful pinkos, no one in the country would seriously doubt that a worldwide slaughter of foreigners would make America safer. While efforts of the heroic Bush administration to wipe out all the Arabs are certainly a good start, we must not forget that other countries in the world are evil and we've got to settle their hash.

Before discussing the litany, it is important to note that this article only provides a tip of the iceberg. Understanding the vital importance of a preemptive foreign policy, we have resolved to establish an institute to rigorously pursue this end. Heading up the International Democratic Institute for Overseas Transplantation (IDIOT) will be a cadre of noted pro-murder libertarians, including Randy Barnett, Deroy Murdock, and Ronald Bailey. Other IDIOT Fellows will include Christopher Hitchens, Rush Limbaugh, Max Boot, Thomas Sowell, and Sean Hannity. With the Institute in place to exhaustively target *all* foreign countries, do not interpret omissions as implying approval.

We do not seek world domination; to this end, we are critical of the Bush administration. We are realists and understand that we will never be able to control some insubordinates. So instead of costly bureaucracy, why not achieve control over the entire globe by eliminating every other

---

[*]October 23, 2006.

inhabitant of it? Half measures will avail us nothing. It is time to own up to the logical implications of our present foreign policy, not cringe at them.

America must become the "terrible swift sword" of the world — a smiter of all evil and ill will. This sword, of course in the form of nuclear warheads, will be directed against the following evildoers (among others):

CHINA — Not only are these people trying to industrialize, but they are hosting the Olympics. Didn't Hitler host the Olympics? By logical deduction then, the Chinese are crypto-Nazis. It's 1938 all over again; we cannot appease Hitler. What's more is that they are trying to be peaceful. Only democracies are allowed to be peaceful. Massive human rights violations obviously warrant massive human rights violations.

CANADA — It is ham; there is no such thing as Canadian bacon. During our first great war, i.e., the French and Indian, they provided comfort to the enemy. Moreover, it has become exceedingly difficult to distinguish Canadians from dull, white Americans. They constitute a natural fifth column, which will one day overrun us. Better safe than sorry.

RUSSIA — They are fooling no one with their "surrender." The breaking up of the Soviet Union was one great political ploy designed at further freezing the Cold War. While we have been navel gazing, the Soviets have been assassinating foreign nationals. It's hard not to admire the KGB, but IDIOT Fellow David Frum cautions us not to ignore "the evidence that the Russian government murdered a British citizen in the British capital with a radiological weapon." Though Frum doesn't go far enough. He says: "If we acknowledged that terrible reality, we would have to do something about it." He fails to understand that if we do the sort of thing neo-conservatives are advocating for Iran, and defending for Iraq, there will be Russians who survive an invasion and conventional bombing.

GERMANY — One word: Hitler. As supreme enemies of liberty, Germans will never change. There are still legions of Holocaust deniers running around spouting their pernicious vitriol and singing "Du Hast." What alternative do we have other than the bomb? Allowing this anti-Semitism to continue would be unconscionable.

VATICAN CITY — Let us not forget that the leader of this country is a theocrat, installed by elitist oligarchs. The Catholic Church is not a democratic institution and dogma is decided upon by gospel missive, not majority.

ISRAEL — Truly a socialist country. As pro-war libertarians, we resent their socialism. The latest chapter in this sorry story is that they have adopted price controls for bread. We'll have to forcibly teach these people that free markets and private property are the last best hope for mankind.

South America — As noted political philosopher Randy Newman points out, "they stole our name" and thus a nuclear first strike is the only appropriate response to this unjust linguistic theft. Yet if the unpatriotic have further doubts, let us not forget that we would not have cocaine, Che tee shirts, and immigrants had it not been for this horrid land.

India — It's now our turn to outsource. Why should Sanjay steal the job of Steve? Because it is more economical and conducive to a global division of labor? Because it engenders world peace? Those things are clearly anti-American. Just as the New Yorker should only purchase goods manufactured within his island or the Peorian only purchase Peorian products, so too should Americans buy American. Exportation is evil, importation, insidious.

Africa — They are continually killing each other in tribal genocidal warfare. Let us help them out, in this regard. Who says we are against foreign aid? No more people means no more genocide — we just choose to drop our foreign aid from 50,000 feet in the air in the form of tactical nuclear warheads.

Syria — This low-lying fruit of a country is ripe, but not for a picking, no, this would imply some sort of desire to govern this veritable Islamofascistan. Who are these Arabs to stand against U.S. aspirations? Let us show them, in the only way these heathens will understand, what it means to mess with the good old U.S.A.

We have the means to kill all these people; we simply lack the will.

George Bush, we implore you to accept our modest proposal! Don't label us as traitors though; you *have* made a valiant effort. But your efforts so far should only be considered the first, timid steps. This is the fundamental problem with neo-conservatism — it's a doctrine that takes too much pleasure in watching death up-close. It is true that our policy will lead to quick, painless extermination, and we can certainly understand the outrage over at *National Review*, but it is the only way. Bush can have his personal pleasure from Iraq, Iran, and Afghanistan, but this is a narrow, limited, and provincial strategy. We are the only true globalists.

Please note: this is another parody.

CHAPTER 6

Let the South Go: St. Abraham's War and Current Foreign Policy*

A century and a half after the war against Southern secession, the foreign policy of our country is still hampered by this tragic event. That is, had the war of federal aggression not taken place, had the South been allowed to leave peacefully, America would be in a far better position to exert a positive direction on several events which trouble the globe at the present time.

This does not imply that a libertarian U.S. foreign policy would include the role of world policeman; organizing non-constitutional standing armies; stationing soldiers abroad in, literally, hundreds of other countries; posting battle ships in every sea and ocean known to man.

No. A proper foreign policy would be informed by George Washington's "Farewell Address" advice: to aim for friendly commercial relations with all nations, but political relations with none; to wish for the safety and happiness of all counties, but to fight to protect only our own.

But this is not to deny that Americans can play a mediating and conciliatory role in foreign affairs. Yes, politicians, bureaucrats and other hirelings of the state would be precluded from any such activities. And this should go for weekends too. After all, they already have full time jobs that

---

*June 20, 2002.

ought to prevent them from gadding about the globe, mixing into other people's business. Executives in private firms are typically contractually prevented from doing anything on their free time incompatible with their full time commitments, and the same ought to apply to government "diplomats."

However, there is nothing in the principles of libertarianism to prevent private citizens from being arbitrators and mediators on the world stage. Surely members of the American Arbitration Association, ex-judges, marriage counselors, etc., could make an important contribution in the direction of putting out some of the many conflagrations now besetting this sorry world.

Except for one thing.

Any American who tried to do so would be engaging in this task with one hand, not to say two, tied behind his back. This is because the clear, obvious, and just (partial) solution to most if not all of the problems of humanity is secession, and this country has a history of repudiating just that sort of occurrence. Nor have we as a society apologized for this moral outrage. Instead, Abraham Lincoln is still seen by most as a sort of secular saint. With the exception of Tom DiLorenzo, Jeff Hummel, David Gordon, Clyde Wilson — and just a very few others — our historians, political scientists, and other intellectuals are still defending the actions of the monster Lincoln. Consider a few examples indicating how such a stance would undermine any efforts at being honest brokers in curing the trouble spots of the earth.

1.   CHECHNYA

Russia is in the midst of fighting a bloody war with this group of individuals, and has been for almost a decade. Tens of thousands of people have been killed. One of them might have invented the cure for cancer.

Is there any reason why the Chechens cannot be allowed to go their separate way? To deny this is especially problematic in view of the fact that some dozens of other former jurisdictions of the former Soviet Union have already been allowed to set up separate countries. What is the relevant difference between Chechnya, on the one hand, and Lithuania, Latvia, Estonia, Belarus, Ukraine, Georgia, Kazakhstan, Turkmenistan, Uzbekistan, Kyrgyzstan, Tajikistan, to say nothing of East Germany, Yugoslavia, Hungary, Croatia, Albania, Poland, Romania, Armenia, the Czech Republic, Slovakia, Serbia, on the other, such that the latter should be allowed to secede and not the former?

One would be hard put to offer any justification for this different treatment. And yet, so deeply embedded is the notion that every country is perfectly constituted, just as it is, at any given time, that maniacal opposition to the departure of this little sliver of land has caused the needless death of thousands of precious human beings.

But could an American advocate the secession of Chechnya? Such a position would be undercut due to our own history with regard to the similar demand on the part of the Confederacy, which was squelched.

2. KASHMIR

India and Pakistan have been at each other's throats for decades over the fate of Kashmir. They have already fought three inconclusive wars to settle this issue. Thousands of precious human beings have perished in these skirmishes. One of them might have composed a symphony, the equal of any of Mozart's. If a nuclear war between these two powers comes about as a result of this dispute, the estimates are that 12 million more will be murdered.

When England left this troubled subcontinent in 1947 the plan that was taken up was that the majority Hindu areas would go to India, and that similarly populated Muslim regions would be amalgamated into Pakistan. As a recipe for peace based on vast and in many cases forced migration, what can be said in behalf of this plan is that there were probably worse alternatives.

But Kashmir was ruled by a Hindu prince. He decided to "give" it to India, despite the fact that the overwhelming majority of residents were Muslim. Pakistan has been trying, ever since, to incorporate this territory on the grounds that it is the rightful owner, and India has been struggling, with equal fervor, to uphold the doctrine that no political separation may ever take place, for any reason.

Now the obvious and just solution is to allow the Kashmiris to secede from India. Then, it could either join Pakistan, or remain as a separate political entity, along the Bangladesh model. But would such a course of action be recommended by any American with a straight face? To ask this question is to answer it.

3. PALESTINE

Jews and Arabs have been slaughtering each other for years in this troubled part of the world. One of these dead, conceivably, might have invented a travel machine or technique that could have allowed us to explore and colonize not only additional planets in this solar system, but in other galaxies as well.

One simple answer to this firestorm is a geographical and political separation of these two peoples. (This would not entirely solve the crisis; there would still remain the issue of which pieces of land would be controlled by which countries, an issue outside our present focus. But such partition would at least be a step in the right direction.)

However, no American, not even a private citizen, could recommend any such plan with clean hands while the Confederate states are still held by the U.S. Colossus. First we have to set straight our own house, before any of us can recommend separation to other jurisdictions, without fear of the justified charge of hypocrisy.

How far should secession go for the libertarian? To ask this is to ask: What is the optimal number of countries in the world? The bottom line answer is, one for each person, or six billion different nations. In the just society, we are each sovereign individuals.

The reigning ideology, of course, makes no such course of action practicable in the present day. But this principle still illuminates the issue, however politically infeasible. It at least establishes a presumption in world affairs: whenever a minority wishes to secede from a majority, they should be allowed to do so. Other things equal, the more countries the better. But more. Minorities should be *encouraged* to break into smaller political entities, if only this will bring us closer to the libertarian ideal number of countries. Further, voluntary separation is part and parcel of freedom of association. The extent to which a person is not free to associate with others of his choosing is the extent to which is he not free but rather a slave.

This principle has no logical, coherent, or ethical stopping point (short, of course, of the libertarian ultimate goal of one person per nation). That is, the seceding country may be, in turn, seceded from. If it is just for the Confederate States to leave the U.S., then it is equally licit for, say, Louisiana to depart from the Confederacy. And if this is legitimate, then it is also proper for Shreveport, for example, to get out from under the control of the Cajun State.

Applied to the Middle East, the result might well be a political archipelago, along the lines of a country comprised of parts of the West Bank and the Gaza Strip, or what is now Pakistan plus Bangladesh, but if this is the will of the people, down to the neighborhood, or, even to the individual level, well then so be it, at least if we want to cleave to any notion of morality.

Certainly, it should be applied to Ireland, to Quebec, to Somalia, and even to the suburbs of the city of Los Angeles.

Secession will not cure all the world's ills, but it will bring us a step closer to this goal. When and if the U.S. ceases to imprison the Confederacy, we will be in a far better position to bring about world peace; or, at least, to help put out many local conflagrations.

II.

Economics

CHAPTER 7

Market vs. State: It Is the Overriding Distinction in Economics and Politics*

J ust as an important difference in everyday life is that between a bathroom and a kitchen, so, too, does a crucial distinction in political-economic philosophy exist between government and private contractual arrangements. But here is where the analogy breaks down. There are other, even more important insights to be garnered in ordinary living than that between these two rooms (e.g., don't eat poison, feed yourself, take care of babies); there is simply *no* more important delineation in libertarian theory than that which exists between coercion (the government) and voluntary cooperation (the market).

Yet, such is the parlous nature of our discipline that there are even people parading themselves around as libertarians who are unaware of this distinction. Worse, there are those who write articles in professional journals, and even books, which are dedicated in their entirety to the obliteration of the difference between the state and private market interaction.

They are not without an argument, paltry as it is. Exhibit "A" in their arsenal is the condominium agreement. These "libertarians" wax eloquent about the severity and comprehensiveness of such housing developments. For example, they typically require that all exteriors be painted in the same color; that fences be identical (e.g., everyone must have, say, a picket fence);

---

*July 19, 2002.

that there be no window air conditioning units. Some even go so far as to stipulate the color of curtains that can be seen from outside, and either compel, or prohibit, such things as floor rugs, Venetian blinds, screen doors, types of foot mats and whether automobiles must, or cannot be, parked in garages. Some prohibit children entirely; others specify minimum ages for residents (e.g., 60 years old for retirement communities). And legion are the rules and regulations concerning noise at which hours, parties, where tricycles can be stored, etc. Compared even to some villages and small towns, the mandates of these private communities can be intrusive, comprehensive, and oft-times arbitrary.

Then, too, there is the fact that both kinds of organizations are typically run on fully democratic principles. And not only that: there is a sense in which, in both cases, it can truly be said that people *agree* to take part in the elections in the first place.

In the case of cooperative housing, this is easy to see. All members of the development sign a purchase contract, indicating willingness to be bound by the condo constitution and by a formula (majority, super majority, whatever) for altering its terms.

For towns, no one, of course, signs the constitution. (If you don't believe this, go back and read Spooner's *No Treason*.) However, argue these "libertarians," by moving into a village the newcomer knows full well the rules of the political entity, or can easily learn them: no spitting on the street, the zoning specifications, speed limits, etc. And, in virtually all cases, town regulations are far less all encompassing than those of condominiums. True, concludes this argument, the city government garners "taxes" while the condo collects membership "fees," but this is a distinction without a difference.

The first chink in this seemingly airtight case can be seen when we examine the position not of the new arrival in town, but rather that of a landowner who was located there before the town was incorporated; or, alternatively, when we look at the plight of the homeowner living just outside the village limits, when it expands to take into its jurisdiction people such as himself living in contiguous but previously unincorporated areas. (We consider the second of these cases not the first, since there are now far more individuals alive who have experienced the latter, not the former.)

So the mayor comes to this homeowner and says to him, "I've got good news for you, Zeke. You're now part of the town. We'll collect your garbage for you, we'll provide city water and sewage services, policing, fire protection, membership in the library; heck, we've even got a municipal swimming pool. You'll have to pay for welfare for the poor, too, of course, but you've always helped your down at their luck neighbors before, so that shouldn't be any burden on you."

Replies Zeke: "That really sounds wonderful. We're really getting modern around her, aren't we, Clem? But I tell you what. I'm going to take a pass on this wonderful opportunity. I see no reason for change. Thanks, but no thanks."

Whereupon responds Mayor Clem: "I don't think I've fully made my position clear. This really isn't your choice. We took a vote on this, and your side lost. You're in, whether you like it or not."

At this point states Zeke: "Hitler came to power through an election. So don't tell me about the ballot box. However, I'll give you one thing, Clem. At least you don't add insult to injury. At least you don't compound naked aggression with outright lying, Clem, like those so called 'libertarians' who see no difference between being amalgamated into a town against their will, and buying into a residential community. Your demand for my tax money was refreshingly honest, albeit a bit brutal, for a person I used to think of as a good neighbor."

So much for the first chink in the armor, the case where the property owner is forcibly incorporated into the town. There is indeed a relevant difference between being compelled to be part of the village, and voluntarily joining the condo.

But what about the stronger case for the "libertarian" side of this argument, the one where a new arrival moves into town, buys a house, etc., knowing full well what rules and taxes he will be bound by? Is it not true that at least in this case, the municipal government is indistinguishable from the strata council that runs the condominium?

Not at all. Consider the following case. I buy a home in a dangerous neighborhood, say, the South Bronx. I know full well that the crime rate there is high, and that I will be especially targeted, given the color of my skin. Perhaps I make this economic decision because of the cheaper real estate, or because I want to be closer to "the people," the better to study their situation and help eradicate poverty. In any case, as soon as I move in, I am confronted by a street thug with a knife who says to me:

"Give me your wallet, you white mother f-----, or I'll cut you, man."

Whereupon I pull out my gun and say to the criminal: "My good man, you are overmatched, firepower wise. Cease and desist from your evil ways, and go about your legitimate business, if you have any."

This street person, who, unbeknownst to me, is actually a bit of a philosopher, expounds as follows: "You don't seem to understand. I'm one of those 'libertarians' who maintain that since you moved to the South Bronx with the full knowledge you would very likely be subjected to muggings of the sort I'm now pulling (or at least trying pull; I've never met a less cooperative victim than you; what's this world coming to?), you in effect have *agreed* to be mugged by robbers like me. So, get with the program, man."

The point is, as we can readily see, the ability to *foresee* an event is not at all equivalent to *agreeing* to it. Yes, I can full well *predict* that if I move to the South Bronx, I'll likely be victimized by street crime. But this is not at *all* the same thing as *acquiescing* in such nefarious activities. Yet, according to the "libertarian" argument we are considering, the two are indistinguishable.

Similarly, the individual who locates in a city with taxes, zoning, etc., can be expected to know he will be subjected to these depredations, just like everyone else there. But this is more than a country mile away from his having *agreed* to be coerced by these evil doers. The new arrival in town no more gives permission for the tax collector to mulct funds from him than does the newcomer to the South Bronx give permission to the mugger to violate his rights.

In very stark contrast indeed, the purchaser of a unit in a housing development not only foresees he will be subjected to a monthly membership payment, and to a welter of restrictions as to what he can do with his property, but actually *consents* to pay the former and be bound by the latter. The proof of this is that he *signs* a bill of sale, stipulating all of the above. In the town-citizen case, there is no such written contract.

It is no exaggeration to say that *the* most important distinction in all of libertarian theory is that between coercion and non-coercion. Obliterate this divergence and there is *nothing* left to libertarianism at all. This is so important, it bears repeating: libertarianism consists of *nothing* more than the implications of this one single solitary distinction. Without it, there is absolutely no theory.

CHAPTER **8**

What Do Boxing and Business Schools Have in Common?: The Problem of Ratings*

It is one thing for pinkos, commies, demopublicans, republicrats, left-ies, neo-cons, etc., to denigrate this distinction. That is, indeed, entirely fitting and proper. If they *didn't* do this, they could hardly be character-ized as I have just done. However, it is quite another thing for "libertar-ians" to make this mistake. They ought to give up this pernicious doctrine, or at least have the decency to stop characterizing themselves as libertar-ians. Everyone knows that the rating of pugilists by the various boxing au-thorities is, how shall we say this, highly problematic.

There are four main boxing associations: the International Boxing Federation (IBF), the World Boxing Association (WBA), the World Boxing Council (WBC) and the World Boxing Organization (WBO). This, alone, seemingly, would be bad enough; the fact that there are numerous other institutional ratings agencies — the International Boxing Association, the International Boxing Council, the International Boxing Organization, the International Boxing Union, the World Boxing Federation, the World Box-ing Union, and FightNews — renders matters utterly chaotic.

But one does not have to resort to these others to show the depths of depravity to which ratings have sunk. The "Big Four" will do fine in this regard, thank you very much.

Consider the following (as of September 5, 2001):

---

*September 27, 2001.

- Mike Tyson is rated first contender by the WBC, 5th by the IBF, 6th by the WBA, and not at all by the WBO.

- Hasim Rahman is the WBC and IBF champ, but does not appear in the top ten of the WBA and WBO.

- The only heavyweights listed as elite in all four rankings are Vitali Klitschko, Lennox Lewis, and David Tua.

- As far as the WBC, WBA, and IBF are concerned, Roy Jones is the best light heavyweight; he is not included in the WBO top ten.

- Bernard Hopkins (WBC, IBF) and Felix Trinidad (WBA) are middleweight champions; but neither is listed even as an also ran by the WBO.

- Only Hector Camacho and Oktay Urkal make the top ten cut for all four Super Lightweights.

- Floyd Mayweather (WBC), Joel Casamayor (WBA), Steve Forbes (IBF), and Acelino Freitas (WBO) all have super featherweight championship belts; but none is so much as mentioned by any of the other three.

- Only Naseem Hamed is a top ten featherweight for all four boxing organizations; Julio Chacon (WBO), Frankie Toledo (IBF), Derrick Gainer (WBA) and Erik Morales (WBC) are champs, but none are included as contenders by any of the other big four.

Ok. So the fight game has always been not just a little bit unsavory. But what are we to make of a similar situation with regard to, of all things, graduate schools of business?

There are three widely respected periodicals which rate business schools by ranking them in terms of quality. They are the *Wall Street Journal, Business Week* magazine, and *U.S. News & World Report.* Despite the undoubted prestige of these three, sharp criticisms have been leveled at their treatment of the leading colleges of business.

For example, while Dartmouth College was ranked number one by the *Wall Street Journal,* it garnered only eleventh place as far as *U.S. News & World Report* was concerned, and slipped to sixteenth position in *Business Week*'s compilation.

If these widely disparate ranks for one institution of higher learning were not enough to cast doubt upon the veracity of the ratings, consider the following: the business schools of only Harvard, Chicago, Northwestern, and

Michigan made top ten on the hit parade of all three magazines. None of the other preeminent places, not Stanford, not Yale, not the Wharton School at the University of Pennsylvania, were posted in this category by all three sets of journalists.

Worse, not a one of these supposedly objective newspapers placed my own school, the Joseph A. Butt, S.J., College of Business at Loyola University New Orleans, in any of their top ten places.

However, something deeper than mere sleaze would appear to account for these obvious errors. The rankings disparity, as can be seen, is by no means limited to the "sweet science." Further, *Consumer Reports* does not always agree with *Good Housekeeping*, and the two of them are often out of step with yet other ratings agencies.

The reason for all the diversity stems, ultimately, from the fact that ranking services are a private, for-profit industry. There is competition between firms, and differences of opinion almost necessarily arise in such contexts.

Some people call for the government to intervene in such circumstances, to rationalize matters, to bring order out of the chaos.

But this would be a step in precisely the wrong direction.

Competition always brings a better product than public sector socialism. Yes, things can get messy there, but that is the continually churning market for you. Governments, too, make mistakes (think thalidomide!). We get more and better information from a myriad of sources, than from one monopoly state enterprise.

If you think we should have only one boxing organization under state control, do you think there should be only one governmental magazine rating MBA programs? Such periodicals disagree with one another not just on business college prestige, but with regard to many other things as well. If mere divergence of opinion warranted public sector control, the road to socialism would be greased even the more.

CHAPTER 9

The Motor Vehicle Bureau; Confronting It[*]

Newly arrived in New Orleans from Arkansas, one of the first things I did after settling in was to attempt to register my automobile and get a Louisiana license plate (I can't pass for a native with an out of town vehicle.)

I say "attempt" advisedly, because this quest, as it turned out, was quite a struggle.

On my first try, I went out to the Louisiana Motor Vehicle Bureau in Kenner, a 25-minute trip from my university. I saw a line of about 35 people, and took my place at the end of it. After 20 minutes, only two people had been served. This implied a wait of 330 minutes, or five and a half hours. Not having brought any work to do with me, I scurried back to my office, tail between my legs.

The next day I arrived with sandwiches and a book to read. There were only 20 people ahead of me. Hot diggity, I thought, this would take "only" 200 minutes at yesterday's pace, or a little over 3 hours.

Happily, we were queued up in "snake" formation, instead of the more usual system — popular for public sector "services" — of a group of people waiting, separately, for each clerk. At least I didn't have to worry about being at the slowest moving wicket.

---

*September 12, 2001.

But, did you ever stand around, trying to read a book, cheek by jowl with almost two dozen people, confined, sardine-like, to a space of about 10 feet by 10 feet? It was no picnic for me, and I'm a relatively young pup of only six decades; there were also some really old people on that line. This was cruel and unusual punishment for them.

Why couldn't they give us numbers in order of arrival, and let us sit while we waited? For that matter, why does serving each "customer" take so long? And, if it really does, why not hire a few more clerks, or more efficient ones? Better yet, why not simplify the process? Are the opportunity costs of time of New Orleanians really that close to zero? Are we cattle? If they treated prisoners as badly as that, they would riot.

But the real problem is not with any of these considerations. It is, rather, that there is simply no competition for the provision of licensing and registry services. If there were an alternative (or two) available, I and at least several of my queue-mates would have patronized a competitor with alacrity.

The difficulty is, we have embraced the old Soviet system of economics in our so-called "public" sector. In the bad old U.S.S.R., there were long waiting lines for just about everything. In the land of the free and the home of the brave, we have sovietized such things as the motor vehicle bureau, the post office, and a myriad of other government bureaucracies.

It is time, it is long past time, to privatize these last vestiges of socialism, and allow the winds of free enterprise to blow away these cob-webs of inefficiency. The reason we have reasonably good pizza, toilet paper, and shoes, etc., — and don't have to wait hours for them — is because there is competition in these industries. Those entrepreneurs who cannot cut it are forced to change the error of their ways through our marvelous profit and loss system. If they cannot, they are forced into bankruptcy, and others, more able, are eager to take their places. Adam Smith's "invisible hand" assures quality service wherever competition reigns.

In the event, my second wait took only an hour and 45 minutes. The queue moved faster than I had thought it would. I was "lucky." (Furious, I wrote this op-ed while waiting in line.) I am now the proud owner of a spanking new Louisiana license plate.

CHAPTER 10

Want To Help the Poor and Oppressed? Encourage Laissez-Faire Capitalism, You Bleeding-Heart Liberal, You*

OPEN LETTER TO THE INTERNATIONAL JUSTICE MISSION

Dear Mr. Haugen:
I attended your speech at Regent College in Vancouver, Canada; I wanted to comment at that time, but the Q&A period was too limited. So I thought I would share my thoughts with you in this format.

If I had to summarize your speech, it was that callous acts are taking place on a massive scale all throughout the world at present, and it is the duty of Christians to try to stop these outrages. In order to do so, religious people should give up their self-centeredness, and increase their rate of charitable donations (both in terms of money and time) toward these ends.

According to Adam Smith, "It is not from the benevolence of the butcher, the brewer or the baker that we expect our dinner, but from their regard to their own interest. We address ourselves not to their humanity but to their self love, and never talk to them of our own necessities but of their advantages."

---

*July 21, 2004.

What I get from this is not that benevolence does not exist within the human breast. Rather, that it is in very scarce supply. Which means that rational men will want to economize on this rare and precious flower, instead of advocating that it be used promiscuously; realizing it will always be in short supply, instead of thinking it can be radically expanded.

And, there are good and sufficient sociobiological reasons why this should be so. Why we as a species are "hard wired" in this direction. If there were a tribe of cave men who were not primarily interested in number one, virtually to the exclusion of everyone else, they would have long ago died off. Better yet, if this theoretical tribe focused their limited benevolence widely, instead of narrowly, to their family members, friends, and neighbors, they would have gone extinct. We are descended from folk like those; that is why we are the way we are, in the main. Yes, there are some very few exceptions, but they only prove the general rule. We are focused on our narrow little lives, because this was required by our ancestors, as a matter of survival.

I entirely agree with your goals: to reduce or better yet eliminate the massive viciousness that now plagues us, such as the mass murder, slavery, etc., you mentioned so eloquently. But your means toward this end, increasing the level of benevolence in society, and widening its focus, I think are doomed to failure based on these considerations.

You may not have noticed, but all the countries you mentioned as examples of brutality were underdeveloped or retrogressing ones (you called them "developing countries" but that is just a bit of misleading political correctitude you might consider jettisoning). This leads to an alternative means toward eradicating the cruelty: economic development. Happily, Adam Smith again rides to the rescue. The full title of his most famous book is *An Inquiry into the Nature and Causes of the Wealth of Nations*. His recipe for economic development was, in a nutshell, with some slight reservations: laissez faire capitalism. Murray N. Rothbard, my own mentor, goes much further, and criticizes Adam Smith himself for deviating too widely from this proper goal of full economic freedom in *The Logic of Action: Applications and Criticism from the Austrian School.*

The idea was that government which governs least governs best. Some of my research empirically supports the contention that economic freedom leads to prosperity and appears in *Economic Freedom of the World*, 1975–1995 (with James Gwartney and Robert Lawson). Given that greater wealth reduces man's inhumanity to man, this is a course of action that should not be overlooked by you and your organization.

It is my contention that if your claim is true that to be a good Christian one must make an effort to stop the massive evils you mentioned, then it is no less true that it is also incumbent upon you to learn why some nations are rich while others are desperately poor. An aphorism might come in handy, here: "Don't fight the alligators, drain the swamp." You are fighting alligators; attempting to rescue little Marie or David or Jose. This is all well and good. I salute you for this. Someone has got to do this, as these injustices cry out to the heavens for redress. And, there is such a thing as specialization and the division of labor. But I think you should recognize that there is *another* and, yes, a *better* and more all-encompassing means toward this end: economic development based on free enterprise.

I emphasize this not so much because of what you said in your formal lecture, which ignored the points I am making, but based on your answer to the very last question asked of you. It was posed by a young lad who I took to be a Regent College seminary student, since his remarks were based on the usual Marxist claptrap taught in such establishments of higher learning. He asked if you were not concerned with systemic problems such as the "economic violence" based on unequal income distribution. (I don't remember this verbatim, but this was the essence of his stance.) His implication was that western countries ought to increase their level of foreign aid to underdeveloped nations. But this is economic illiteracy of the highest order, as the work of Peter Bauer has stressed over and over again. Instead of verbally slapping down this young man as he richly deserved, you bought into his basic premises, but excused yourself from acting on his principles, properly I thought, on the grounds of the need for specialization and the division of labor. But his socialist premises were wrong, and if implemented, will *increase* not decrease, the level of brutality in these poor countries.

Now, I admit that there are also good and sufficient sociobiological reasons why free markets are not now the order of the day. If free markets were the normal, we would all be living in a laissez faire paradise. (It is my contention that in the caveman days, we became altogether too hard wired into following the orders of the tribal chief. Also, since we lived in very small communities compared to the present day, only direct cooperation seeped into the genetic pool. Cooperating indirectly, through gigantic markets, has come far too late in the history of our species to have been incorporated into our genes.) But this is no reason for intellectuals such as yourself to accept the siren song of socialism.

The rich western countries do not really need capitalism that much; this system in the past has set up the capital, and the legal system, to ensure relative wealth, and thus little internal mass murder. It is the poor nations in Africa and elsewhere that are in the greatest need of free enterprise. Thanks to their enjoyment of relative economic freedom for many years, the capitalist west can now afford a modicum of pernicious socialism. In contrast, free enterprise being virtually unknown in the third world, socialist egalitarianism is the death knell of their economy.

In closing, one last criticism of your presentation: lose that film clip showing a child buyer being tied up by the police. You may not have noticed it, but it also showed a television set in the background. This implies electricity, and a certain minimal level of prosperity — all totally incompatible with your story of people selling their kids motivated by dire poverty.

I hope you take these remarks in the spirit I mean them: as an attempt to help you with your very good works.

Mr. Gary Haugen did not see fit to respond to this open letter.

CHAPTER   11

Want To Cure Poverty? Get the Government Out of the Market*

Louisiana Governor Blanco is now holding hearings on the problem of poverty. Since she is a mainstream politician, she will likely arrive at the wrong answers for its cause and adopt fascistic solutions for its cure. Worse, this initiative will cost hundreds of thousands of dollars or more and thus exacerbate the very poverty she is supposedly fighting.

In 1776 Adam Smith wrote *An Inquiry into the Nature and Causes of the Wealth of Nations*. The governor might do worse than cancel her meetings and read this book instead. Smith said that those countries that rely mainly on the free enterprise system of private property rights and the rule of law prosper, while those that do not are consigned to a life of grinding poverty.

Smith, who was not as free enterprise-oriented as his reputation implies, hedged on this basic insight with too many exceptions and too many concessions to government, but the general rule he articulated was as true in the eighteenth century as it is in our own and applies as much to countries as to states and cities.

Why do markets work to alleviate poverty and governments fail?

The main reason is the profit and loss system, the automatic feedback loop mechanism of free enterprise. If an entrepreneur does a bad job, people

---

*February 23, 2005.

avoid his firm. If he does not mend the error of his ways, bankruptcy is the inevitable and usually swift result. In sharp contrast, if a politician makes mistakes in satisfying a constituency, he can stay in office for up to four years; a bureaucrat, practically forever.

The situation regarding pizza, pens, and pickles is pretty satisfactory; those who could not provide these goods at a competitive quality and price went broke. But what of the post office and the motor vehicle bureau? Poor service for decades, and nothing we consumers can do about it.

Why do free markets tend toward income equality? The only legitimate way to earn vast sums of money under free enterprise is by enriching others. Yes, Bill Gates, Sam Walton, Henry Ford and Ray Kroc make billions, but they do so by economically uplifting all those they deal with. If people did not benefit from dealing with Microsoft, Wal-Mart, Ford, and McDonalds, they would not continue to do so.

In contrast, in politics, vast fortunes are made not by attracting customers but by raising taxes and siphoning off the lion's share of them. The wealth of the politician rises, and that of everyone else falls.

But do governments not give money to the poor in the form of welfare? Doesn't that help the poor? First, only the crumbs go to the poor. The rich, after all, run the government. It would take quite a bit more benevolence than they have for them to orchestrate things against their own interests.

Second, what little money does go to the poor impoverishes them; it does not lift them out of poverty. The key to understanding the direction of causation in this paradoxical situation is the family: Anything that supports this vital institution reduces poverty; anything that undermines it increases poverty.

Family breakdown is causally related to all sorts of poverty indices besides lack of money: imprisonment, lack of educational attainment, unemployment, lower savings, illegitimacy, etc.

And what is the effect of welfare on the family? To ask this is to answer it. As Charles Murray has shown in his insightful book *Losing Ground*, the social worker makes a financial offer to the pregnant girl that the father of her baby cannot even come close to matching. But they do so on the condition that this young man be out of the picture. A recipe for family disaster if ever there was one.

Slavery was not able to ruin the black family (poverty is disproportionately a black problem), but insidious welfare had that very effect. The black family was just about as strong as the white in the years following the War of Northern Aggression, but fell apart after Johnson's War on Poverty.

Similarly, social security weakens intergenerational family ties. Public housing, with its income cutoff points, evicts intact families. The remaining female heads of families are no match for gangs of teenage boys lacking adult male role models.

The government is also a direct source of poverty. Its minimum wage and union legislation makes it difficult if not impossible for poor youth to get jobs. Its rent control makes cheap housing scarce. Its tariffs make all basic necessities more expensive, and its subsidies to business have the same effect.

Want to cure poverty, Governor Blanco? Reduce government interference with the free enterprise system.

CHAPTER 12

Airport Insecurity*

L ast week, I took an airplane from Vancouver to Atlanta, to give some lectures at the Mises Institute. I took a cab to the airport, since I would be away from my summer home for over two weeks, and this would be cheaper than parking the car at the airport for all that time. I had in my possession a letter, with a Canadian stamp on it, that I really wanted to get out into the socialist mail system. I had intended to mail it the day before, but in the rush of traveling, I had forgotten all about it, until I arrived at the airport.

Happily, there was a post office box right there at the airport, and I dropped the letter into it. But, then a thought occurred to me: this facility was one of those where you pull down a little door like contraption, put the letter in, close the door to make sure the letter was indeed posted, and then close it one last time. Although I only place in it a thin letter the opening was wide enough to mail off a package of a size sufficient to hold 3–4 hard cover books, or maybe a half dozen paper backs. Whereupon it suddenly hit me, far more disquieting: the opening was sufficient, more than sufficient, for a terrorist to place a bomb, a reasonably big one, into that container. He would not have even had to commit suicide to do so. A weight of explosives small enough to fit into that opening could have done a powerful lot of damage, murdering dozens if not scores of people in a crowded airport. Timed to explode ten minutes later, the perpetrator could have gotten off scot free.

---

*April 1, 2005.

Then, I noticed something else. Although I had to ask directions for the location of the post office box, the same was not true for trash cans. They were literally all over the place, in plain sight, dozens of them placed every 20 yards or so, as far as the eye could see. Each of them, in this particular airport, had a circular hole at the top, measuring more than my hand span (about 8 inches). These were in effect an open invitation to our friends from the terrorist community.

I thought about sharing this information with any one of the myriad of guards, busy bodies, uniformed gropers, policemen, checkers, x-ray people, who infest a modern airport. I did not do so for several reasons. One, although I had plenty of time before my scheduled departure (one of the "conveniences" of modern air travel is that you have to waste an inordinate amount of time arriving early), I anticipated the reaction of any of these worthies to whom I might confide my apprehension about post office boxes and waste receptacles, along the following lines: "Come with us, please." Whereupon I would have been detained for hours at best, and days in jail at worst, for intensive questioning. "What business are you in?" "Have you ever published or said anything critical of the government?" ("Me? Certainly not," might not have been able to withstand even the most cursory of scrutiny in such circumstances.) "Why are you so concerned about bombing?" "Are you a terrorist?" "Do you know anyone from Iraq?" "Do you profess the Muslim faith?"

As I say, speaking up in this public-spirited way would have made me miss the plane, or worse. Instead, I started writing up this column in the airport, while awaiting my departure. Paranoid that I am, I am now keeping my eyes peeled for shifty looking characters putting packages in waste cans (there being no post office boxes in sight, I'm not worried about them). I'm also worried about minions of the state. I am also busily looking over my shoulder as I write, making sure no one is looking at what I write, attempting to decipher my handwriting (I write by hand in airports and later type up what I have written).

But here I'm relatively safe. I can barely read my own handwriting. Then, too, there is something off-putting to me about aiding and abetting these inept airport guardians of ours. They are agents of an institution Spooner has called "a band of murderers and thieves."

While I have no doubt that were I to see one of them drowning I would toss him a life raft (heck, I am an excellent swimmer with life guard training, I would probably jump in to save him even at some risk to my own life), I would do so only out of appreciation of our common humanity. I would do so despite his role as an agent of the state apparatus. Here, did I but make any suggestion to the police about postal boxes and trash cans being an invitation to terrorists, I would have been helping them in precisely this role. As I say, off-putting.

Why are these morons so stupid? Why do our "protectors" pat us down and search for, of all things, nail clippers? Why do they adopt the identical procedures at every airport? Do they not realize that this makes it easier for the bad guys? Why do they act so as to make it prudent for us to get to the airport two hours before a flight, wasting zillions of man-hours? Why don't they focus their attention on young men of Arabic appearance, who have been responsible for a very high proportion of all such incidents?

This is surely due to a combination of political correctness run amuck, and to monopoly operation. As to the former, I once in a beknighted mood thought it would disappear under the pressure of life and death situations. Not so, not so. The evil Red Cross accepted blood donations from homosexuals without testing them for fear of offending them, and thereby infected with the AIDS virus hundreds of hapless and trusting hemophiliacs. And now, the forces of political correctness would rather see innocents blown to smithereens rather than engage in eminently justified racial (sexual, and age) profiling.

As it happens, however, looking askance at young male Arabs in airports and other such sensitive places is no such thing. It is, rather, criminal profiling. It would only be racial profiling if inspectors subjected to heightened security, say, Arab grandmothers, who have not at all been linked to terrorist acts. Why do airport security guards target young attractive women? (Okay, okay, we all know the answer to that one.)

The other element is lack of competition. Why is this so important? Well, there are imbeciles, also, in the private sector of the economy. Grocers who don't wash their floors. Filling stations located on cul-de-sacs. Restaurants whose chefs can't cook their way out of a paper bag. But what happens with such ineptitude? The market's system of profit and loss, or weeding-out firms that cannot cut the mustard, is the difference between the two very, very different sectors of the economy.

Idiocy in the private sector exists, but it is continually being pared away. No such fail-safe mechanism underlies and supports government enterprise. Imagine if safety protection at airports were run under the free market sector, and one firm, the ACME agency, paid great attention to nail clippers and black grandmothers, but ignored garbage cans and Arab males of a certain age. There is a name for such companies, and the name is "bankrupt." They would be eliminated, forthwith, through the competitive process.

It does not matter that our homeland security people wear uniforms. Or must pass civil service types of exams, where they answer theoretical questions theoretically. Or are forced to attend training sessions, where they see films of past events. There is simply no automatic mechanism that continuously improves quality, as occurs every day in the market place. We do not owe our reasonably good pizzas, shoes, and bicycles to geniuses. Rather, to this weeding-out system.

The people supposedly protecting us from terrorists at airports are cut from the same cloth as those who run the motor vehicle bureaus, the post office, and the alphabet soup regulatory agencies. Try reasoning with the denizens of these organizations.

I do not say that nothing will ever be done about potential dangers posed by the receptacles at airports. Even without a market system, common sense may yet prevail. But don't hold your breath.

Maybe I should shut up about this entire topic. Maybe I should not be raising this particular safety issue, lest the terrorists add this new technique to their repertoire. After all, I am a member of the air-traveling public, and I have many loved ones who are, too. I thought about that. But, I believe that the terrorists are smarter than the air safety bureaucrats. If I publicize this potential danger in the manner I am now doing, maybe this threat will become officially recognized, anticipated, and dealt with: no receptacles of this type in airports any more. Or, maybe fully transparent ones.

On the other hand, if I keep silent about it, the murderers of innocents will undoubtedly adopt it. But in publicizing the matter, am I not violating my own principles, or, at least, my revulsion at supporting the government? No, I am not. There is all the world of difference between public speaking, or writing in a format such as the present one, knowing full well that agents of the state can access such information and analysis, on the one hand, and, on the other, helping them directly, for example by mentioning this concern to one of their ilk at an airport, or directly consulting with them on such a matter, whether for pay or not.

Take an analogy. In the next year or so, a book of mine on privatizing highways will be published. In it I state that a competitive system for roadways would likely engage in peak load pricing that would radically decrease traffic congestion, and would institute a number of safety devices which would greatly reduce highway fatalities. Will the authorities read this book and implement some of these suggestions? Possibly. This will not stop me from publication. But was I actually to consult with the National Highway Traffic Safety Administration, as does an otherwise libertarian Reason Foundation, then I would, in my own opinion, be acting inconsistently with this philosophy.

I take that back. Did my "consulting" with them consist of no more than telling them to disband, and privatize all roads, streets, highways, etc., then that would be entirely compatible with the libertarian philosophy.

The other day I received a telephone phone call from the State Department of the U.S. They wanted to consult with me about how best to improve the Iraqi economy. I mentioned a consulting fee of $400 per hour, and not an eyelash was batted. Then, I said that I would consult with them only on the topic of the immediate withdrawal of all U.S. personnel from that country, since I opposed their incursion. The spokesman's response was to politely hang up. But suppose he had persisted. Would I have acted improperly as a consultant? I think not, as long as I advocated nothing incompatible with libertarianism.

B. Macroeconomics

CHAPTER 13

Keep the Penny, Toss the Fed: On the Criminals Who Killed This Once-Useful Coin[*]

For some people, benighted souls, the passing of the copper-colored penny coin is long overdue. "Good riddance to bad rubbish," they might say. After all, this bit of metal hardly buys anything, nowadays. Ubiquitous on the counters of shops around the country are cups holding pennies, there for the use of customers in order to help them make change. But a coin given away for free, these people might argue, can hardly be counted upon to conduct the nation's business. To a great extent pennies just weigh down pockets and pocketbooks, and the sooner they are gone, the fewer tailor bills and pocketbook repair costs will be required.

There is no doubt that these people are correct. Using the penny to conduct today's business is like a car with a rumble seat (don't know what that is youngster? go look it up) or riding around in a horse and buggy. Strictly of antiquarian interest.

And yet, and yet …

'Twas not so long ago that the penny could pull its full financial weight. When I was a youngster in the 1940s, no one dared condescend to this coin. For a very few of them, one could purchase an ice cream cone, a comic book, a candy bar, or even a ticket to a matinee movie. Some restaurants featured menus from the early days of the turn of the last century (for those

---

[*]August 29, 2001.

who have been Rip Van Winkling it for the last few years, I'm referring to 1899) when a penny was a robust coin indeed. A corporal's guard of them would entitle someone to pretty much an entire meal.

What has happened? Why is it that the penny, to say nothing of the nickel, dime, quarter, 50 cent piece, and even, truth be told, the dollar (which will soon follow into oblivion), don't seem to amount to very much in terms of purchasing power? In a word, it is all due to inflation. And who, in turn, is responsible for this reprehensible state of affairs? It is the government, specifically the Treasury Department and the Federal Reserve System (since 1913), which have together conspired against the public interest. They have done so in effect by creating more money, at a faster rate of increase than that enjoyed by the goods and services we create. Too much money chasing too few products yields higher prices, the opposite side of the coin (excuse the pun) of inflation.

There used to be a TV series featuring the "T" men. Every week they would walk down a set of stairs, and attempt to bring to justice the counterfeiters who were responsible for inflating the currency. Had there been better (well, more accurate writers) they would have turned around, marched back up those steps, and arrested their bosses.

For before the advent of statist money, when people were free to choose the means to intermediate their financial affairs, they had typically resorted to gold (sometimes silver). There has been no inflation at all in terms of gold. Centuries ago one could purchase an expensive suit of clothes for an ounce or two of this metal, and the same applies today.

The only reason governments horned in on this essentially free enterprise industry was to disguise their insatiable, greedy, and excessive demands for our money. They have only three ways of raising funds: taxes, borrowing, and inflating the currency. But they are widely and properly reviled when they resort to the first two to excess. The third alternative is embraced by them because the causes of inflation are so well hidden from the public that the blame for it can be readily placed on businessmen and workers.

Yes, the penny is now obsolete. But rather than getting rid of it, we should instead throw out those rascals in Washington who have so debased it. Then we should return to the gold standard (three decades ago the evil Nixon tore asunder our last ties to this system), and once again allow the penny to take its rightful place as the conductor of small scale — but important — commerce. Don't throw out this coin! Toss out Alan Greenspan and his Fed instead.

CHAPTER 14

Private Enterprise and the Fed; What Should Be the Relationship?*

Several years ago I attended a meeting of the Association of Private Enterprise Educators (APEE).[1] This group was initially started by a group of holders of free enterprise chairs at various universities (I suppose I now qualify under that rubric) but membership had been long before open to all those academics and other scholars who favor, and work for the promotion of, free enterprise and economic freedom. (This is my own description of that group, but I doubt that any member of it would object.)

Much to my surprise, and even dismay, the high point of the program, the plenary after dinner speech, was given by a member of the Dallas Fed, who described his organization as the "free-enterprise" Fed. I also learned that this organization was one of the major financial supporters of APEE, or at least of that particular meeting.

This gave me pause for thought, to say the least. At the conclusion of his speech, skunk at the garden party style, during the question and answer

---

[1] The criticisms of APEE mentioned below concern that organization solely as it functioned in 1996–1998, the only period of my experience with them. They are entirely irrelevant to the organization as it is now constituted.

*January 10, 2003.

period, I got up on my hind legs and declaimed that this was more than passing curious. How is it possible to reconcile participation of the Fed, any Fed, in a group ostensibly devoted to laissez faire capitalism? Would not the money supply in an economically free country consist of something chosen by market participants, for example, gold, rather than of fiat currency imposed, from above, by government of all institutions, of which the Fed was part?

I also appended to my remarks a gratuitous, or, perhaps, not so gratuitous attack on Alan Greenspan, for having known these truths during his Randian days, for still claiming free enterprise credentials, and yet continuing to preside over the Fed. In response the speaker said that Greenspan could defend himself — a reasonable enough proposition, I suppose — followed by a litany of all the great free enterprise things done by the Dallas Fed — which I thought very much beside the point.

My queries were met by stunned silence from the crowd. There were no publicly made follow up supportive questions or comments from the audience. Only one person approached me afterward, with support for my position.

In the intervening years, I have had time to reflect upon this curious situation, and hence a few thoughts.

1. The "free enterprise" of APEE as constituted in the nineties did not extend so far as to include money, macroeconomics, business cycles, etc. APEE espoused a rather narrow conception of economic liberty. Were there many members of the group who included such issues in their vision of the free marketplace, they would likely either cutoff affiliations with the Fed or at the very least have speakers advocating free enterprise in this realm. It would be unlikely in the extreme that they would highlight a Fed speaker in this manner, with no opposition on the program.

2. Is it even compatible with libertarianism for APEE to accept funds from a tainted statist agency such as the Fed? Although this will be controversial within libertarian circles, I maintain that it is.

Let us consider this under two rubrics: deontology, or strict libertarian theory on the one hand, and what might be called libertarian utilitarianism (will an act promote liberty) on the other.

Under the latter category, better that these monies go to APEE which is a pretty good organization all things considered (apart from this one lacuna), than to conduct ordinary Fed business, that is, to further debauch the currency. On the other hand, publicly accepting money from this source sends out a mixed message to the citizenry. It implies that there is nothing incompatible between laissez faire capitalism and government involvement in the money supply.

What about pure libertarian principle? Is it illegitimate to ever accept, or even to seize government property, money, or wealth? Yes, certainly, it is. Ragnar Danneskjold, a fictional character in Ayn Rand's *Atlas Shrugged*, did precisely this. Of course, this was only the first in a two-part act; the second of which was to return the, not stolen but rather liberated money, to its rightful owner, in this case Hank Reardon, representing for present purposes victimized taxpayers.

What about acquiring government property and not returning it to its rightful owner, either keeping it or destroying it? Yes, surely, this, too. Let us first consider keeping it, not returning it. Is such a person a thief, and therefore acting incompatibly with libertarian principles, per se? No. A robber is by definition someone who grabs property from the rightful owner.

The government in this scenario cannot possibly qualify in that regard. Rather, the position occupied by APEE in this scenario (or anyone who accepts a pay check from a statist entity such as a public university, or even from a private university which, in turn, accepts such largesse, or anyone who walks on a public street, or uses the post office) is not that of a thief, since he is by stipulation taking money or property from a wrongful owner.

C. Environmental Economics

CHAPTER 15

Heroic Hunt Farms*

Quick, why do you call left-wing environmentalists watermelons? Because while they are green on the outside, they are also red on the inside.

No better illustration of this political mindset can be seen in the controversy involving hunt farms in Canada. In these game ranches—now legal only in Alberta, Saskatchewan, and Quebec, they have just been banned in neighboring Montana — fees are charged to customers who shoot deer, elk, and sometimes other such trophy animals.

But the watermelons are livid at the prospect. A spokesman for the International Fund for Animal Welfare is trying to ban these enterprises in Alberta and Saskatchewan as his next target. The group People for the (so-called) Ethical Treatment of Animals considers these game farm practices cruel and immoral. Other left-wing environmentalists characterize them as lacking any challenge, akin to shooting fish in a barrel.

But what is it with this emphasis on sportsmanship, of all things? Cows, chickens, sheep, and pigs are not given a "fair chance" to escape from the "hunt" in the stockyards of the nation. If hunters want a sure thing, why should this be of any concern to those claiming to be advocates for the environment?

Are these watermelons in favor of playing games by the rules or preserving endangered species? If the former, then they should cease and desist all further fund raising activities, for these are intrinsically fraudulent.

---

*August 3, 2001.

In any case, *all* hunting, whether on game farms or in the wild, is necessarily unfair, at least when done with guns. To make it a real sporting event, even bows and arrows give the humans too great an advantage. In athletic games, the goal is to achieve competition between at least rough equals, so that no one knows, beforehand, who will win. To attain this level of an even playing field, the *homo sapiens* should be allowed no more than short knives with wolves and bears, and animals of their ilk, and nothing more powerful than, say, a baseball bat or a spear with deer and elk. Then, as back in the caveman days, the animals would have a "sporting" chance.

If the latter, then very much to the contrary of their practice, the interest of those presumptively concerned with the environment should be to *protect animals.* Thus, the question to be asked is *not* how big must the private game preserve be so as to allow adequate cover and protection for the animals, but rather whether this process will reduce, or enhance, the chances of survival for these at risk species.

When put in this manner, there can be little doubt of the effect of these enterprises on the long-term survival probability of deer and elk. They will be positive, very much so. For the prices these farmers can charge the hunters will give them every incentive to make sure that their meal tickets never vanish. The going rate for a medium sized elk is $7,500; for a large one, up to $15,000; and for an exceptional bull, no less than $35,000. If there were any farmer foolish enough to allow his "seed corn" to vanish in an orgy of greed for present profits, he would soon enough be forced into bankruptcy. Survival in this industry means, above all, not allowing young female animals, particularly pregnant ones, to be harmed. As in the case of domestic animals, those most at risk are females past child rearing ages, and almost all males. This, in sharp contrast to the hunt for animals in the wild, where just about anything goes.

The free market environmentalist (not an oxymoron) point is that if you want to preserve species, benevolence, even coupled with wise government regulations (when is the last time you saw one of those?) is not enough. If you want to get the job done, as Adam Smith saw over 200 years ago, you have to make it in the financial self-interest of entrepreneurs that this be done.

Nor should this insight on species survival be limited to deer and elk. Not even to bears, wolves, and lions. More exotic animals can also be helped out through the magic of the market, including rhinoceroses and elephants. Yes, the barnyard in these cases might have to be a bit bigger, and the surrounding fences a lot stronger and probably electrified to boot, but game farms for them, too, are the only guarantee we shall continue to have them available to us.

Whales and other fish present a bit of a greater intellectual challenge. But any species that can land one of their own on the moon can surely come up with electrified fences and other aqueous counterparts of barbed wire, to keep a bunch of fish in their places. Only then can private owners of the denizens of the deep have the financial incentive to protect them—at a profit.

With this bit of economic analysis under our belt, what can we make of the efforts of so-called "environmentalists" to oppose hunt farms, a program so clearly in the interest of endangered species survival? In a word, it is hypocritical. It would appear that their hatred for capitalism is stronger than their desire to protect deer and elk. They ostentatiously attempt to hold high the green flag, but their actions belie this, and instead bespeak their internal true red colors.

CHAPTER 16

Me and Hurricane Ivan:
Thanks A Lot, Government*

I first became personally aware of Hurricane Ivan on Monday, September 13, 2004. There were newscasts telling of the havoc it had played, and the lives lost in the Caribbean a few days before, but it didn't dawn upon me until this date that it might visit New Orleans, my home of some three years.

Particularly disturbing was the story of what might happen if Ivan impacted the Crescent City directly: then, since we are perched at the bottom of a geographical bowl, we would be inundated. Large parts of Lake Ponchartrain, our northern neighbor, a bit of the Mississippi River to the south, and also some of the Gulf of Mexico, further to the south, would land in our laps. In this worst case scenario the water level would rise to about 20 feet, higher than many buildings in town. The dikes and pumps would not be able to handle such an onslaught. I reside on the seventh floor of my building, but my home would be commandeered by those living below. Electricity would of course not be available, and New Orleans is pretty hot and humid in September. Worse, the water would be percolated through with toxic wastes from the numerous refineries nearby, by oil, and by alligators, fire ants, and water snakes, I kid you not.

I was told by several old-time dwellers in this city that this was an unlikely occurrence. Much more probably the storm would miss us by miles,

---

*September 20, 2004.

but that we would still likely lose electricity, and I would be advised to stock up on water, canned food, and flashlight batteries. Not a very pleasing scenario, even if the worst of this disaster passed us by.

Estimated time of arrival of this hurricane: Thursday morning, September 16. Naturally, I thought of retreating to higher ground, along with most other townsfolk. I tried to get a flight out of the local airport on the next day, Tuesday, but nothing was available. There were some standby flights available later that night, but I literally couldn't get to within ten miles of the airport, traffic was so heavy. (Further complicating the airport situation was that it had high-rise parking, taken up not only by air travelers, but also by locals fearing drowned automobiles.)

The announcement was made that the New Orleans Airport would be shutdown as of Wednesday morning, September 15. I made travel arrangements in Houston, Texas (ordinarily about 6 hours away by car) and Lafayette, Louisiana (some 2.5 hours away) for late afternoon Wednesday, September 15, and set out to reach either of them at around 4 a.m. that day. However, I soon experienced literally bumper-to-bumper traffic, and was informed on the radio that this would hold all the way west to the Texas border. It took me some seven hours to reach Baton Rouge, where I had no plane reservation (ordinarily, a 90 minute trip) by dint of some heavy lane-switching New York City-type driving. Luckily, at 11 a.m. I was able to purchase a ticket on the spot for that afternoon, and spent the next few days in Seattle.

It is likely that hurricanes are on the minds of many people in New Orleans, what with the near miss of Ivan, and Jeanne in the offing. Floridians, too, experienced a spot of bad weather. However, hurricanes are only the tip of the iceberg, so to speak: there are also typhoons, earthquakes, lightening strikes, tornadoes, tidal waves, storms, cyclones, monsoons, and just plain old bad weather. All of them are a pain in the butt, and dangerous to boot. These catastrophes are all the fault of — wait for it — government. Had the voracious state not gobbled up oh, about 40 percent of the annual GDP for the last half century or so (in Western Europe, the figure is more like 50 percent), it is likely that mankind would have made at least some progress not merely anticipating these cataclysms, and plotting their future paths, but, also, stopping them from occurring in the first place.

Needless to say, this prediction cannot be definitive. It is extremely difficult to analyze contrary-to-fact conditionals such as these. All we can say for sure are first, richer is safer: the more wealth in a society, the better able the people who comprise it are to figure out a way to ward off natural disasters (and unnatural ones too). Second, governments have instead wasted these vast amounts of monies on killing their own citizens (R.J. Rummel puts the figure on this at almost 200 million in the last century), warred with others of their ilk (at the cost of hundreds of millions of more lives), and engaged in various and sundry welfare type schemes (for example, social "security," socialized medicine, and economic regulation) which have reduced economic growth and development, played havoc with economic incentives, and undermined private property rights and economic freedom, the last best hope for humanity.

So, gentle reader, the next time you are stuck in traffic attempting to escape from one of these conflagrations, remember who, really, is likely at fault. It is your friendly neighborhood local government, along with those in the state capital, and with them the denizens of the *federales*.

Now, there are those, benighted souls, who resist this eminently reasonable economic analysis. They might attempt *reductios ad absurdum* such as: "I guess Hong Kong, which was one of the most ardent supporters of free markets, was able to prevent typhoons and other such natural disasters."

Let me say the following in response to such an objection. Surely, it cannot be denied that hurricane prevention (not mere tracking) is a normal good, forgive the economic jargon. That is, the richer is the society, the more likely it is to want and get this service. Therefore, it follows, logically, that the richer we are, the more likely, or the sooner, we are to have this service of natural disaster prevention.

Let us stipulate that the government spends some 40–50 percent of Gross Domestic Product. If it did not do so, we would be far richer, *ceteris paribus*. It may be that under free enterprise, we would get full hurricane, etc., prevention in "only" 100 years from now, while under the semi-socialist fascist system we now have we would have to wait 200 years for it. Who knows? Stopping these things, cold in their tracks, I admit, is tough to do. But, it is a matter of pure economic logic to say that this happy day will come sooner, *ceteris paribus*, the richer we are, and that government is a drag on the economy. QED.

This does not at all imply that Hong Kong, a very small country, even when it was (relatively) free, would have by now discovered a cure for these natural disasters (or for cancer, or AIDS, or whatever); only that a free Hong Kong is *more likely* to have done so, at any given time, than a less free Hong Kong.

Second objection: an individual cannot expect to earn a profit from good hurricane forecasting, let alone stopping one from starting in the first place. There is a classic free rider problem here. The benefits are so widespread whoever could stop such natural disasters from taking place could not exclude non-payers from enjoying them.

Here is my reply: we already have hurricane forecasting, not all of it provided by government. This demonstrates that the market has overcome the so-called free rider "market failure" problem. The free enterprise system has not seen fit to "exclude" non-payers. Rather, entrepreneurs give it away for free, sometimes as a loss leader; sometimes it serves the function of advertising.

If I knew how to stop Ivan (at very low cost) I would be the most popular man on the planet. Surely, I could find a way to turn that to my financial advantage without threatening that if I were not paid off, I would desist. There is no doubt I would win a Nobel Prize in physics, or some such. Without question private foundations would give me millions to get further discoveries out of me.

There is a whole libertarian-Austrian literature on the difficulties with the free rider argument. The interested reader is encouraged to access it.

CHAPTER 17

Me and Katrina: Weather Socialism*

Here I was, sitting in my office at Loyola University, New Orleans, where I teach economics, very busy doing what I take to be the Lord's work, and something unlikely as a wind on steroids rends asunder my work and life. It presented the denizens of New Orleans with a stark choice. Evacuate at great inconvenience and run the risk that the oncoming bad weather will veer elsewhere rendering such flight unnecessary, or stay put and brazen it out, and have to deal with flooding, lack of electricity, no air conditioning in 90-degree-plus temperatures, to say nothing of actually loss of life and/or limb, either due to the storm itself, or to the aftermath, including looting, flooding, and loss of law and order.

My own *modus operandi*, finely honed after spending almost half a decade in New Orleans, has been to wait until the very last minute, and then bolt out of here, tail between my legs, and then sit in bumper-to-bumper traffic. For Ivan, I crept to Baton Rouge, a trip of a little over an hour in ordinary circumstances, in nine hours. For Katrina, I left home early Sunday afternoon (August 28) inched up to Vicksburg in eight hours, which would usually take a little over two hours. Then, I went on up to Little Rock, my previous stamping ground (actually, it was Conway, a town of about 50,000, which lies about 30 miles northwest of the capital of Arkansas), and from there to Vancouver by plane.

---

*September 3, 2005.

I am now safely ensconced in western Canada, writing up the notes I took en route. Happily, I escaped lightly, without too much inconvenience. But my heart goes out to those who were very much less fortunate.

What has this to do with political economy, the usual subject of my writing interest? A lot, that's what.

I. PRIVATE ENTERPRISE

First of all, the levees that were breached by the hurricane were built, owned, and operated by *government*. Specifically, by the Army Corps of Engineers. The levees could have been erected to a greater height. They could have been stronger than they were. The drainage system could have operated more effectively. Here, the New Orleans Sewerage and Water Board was at fault. It consists of three main operating systems: sewerage, water, and drainage. Had they been, a lot of the inconvenience, fright, and even loss of life undergone in this city could have been avoided.

Then, too, these facilities may have fooled many people into thinking they were safer than they actually were. I know this applies to me. Thus, people were in effect subsidized, and encouraged to settle in the Big Easy. Without this particular bit of government mismanagement, New Orleans would likely have been settled less intensively. (On the other hand, at one time this city was the largest in the South; statist negligence of a different kind — graft, corruption, over-regulation — is responsible for it having a smaller population than otherwise.)

I am not appalled with these failures. After all, it is only human to err. Were these levee facilities put under the control of private enterprise, there is no guarantee of zero human suffering in the aftermath of Katrina. No, what enrages me is not any one mistake, or even a litany of them, but rather the fact that there is no automatic feedback mechanism that penalizes failure, and rewards success, the essence of the market system of private enterprise.

Will the New Orleans Sewerage and Water Board suffer any financial reverses as a result of the failure of their installations to prevent the horrendous conditions now being suffered by New Orleanians? To ask this question is to answer it.

One crucial step forward then, would be the privatization of this enterprise as part of the rebuilding process (if that indeed occurs; for more on this, see below). Perhaps a stock company could be formed; I suspect that the largest hotels, restaurants, universities, hospitals and other such ventures would have an incentive to become owners of such an enterprise.

Right now, the levees are run by the very same types of folks responsible for the post office and the motor vehicle bureau. I takes no position on whether levees are a good or bad thing; only that if they are to be built, this should be done by an economic entity that can lose funding, and thus put its very existence at risk, if it errs. This can only apply to the market, never the state.

This is neither the time nor place to examine in detail the case for private ownership of bodies of water such as the Mississippi River, Lake Ponchartrain, and, indeed, all oceans, rivers, seas, and lakes. But the same principles apply here as they do to land. Suffice it to say that this is a question that should be explored, for it is no accident that where there is private property there is safety and responsibility, and where there is not there is no responsibility.

Second, numerous roads, highways, and bridges were washed out, collapsed, or were swept away. This makes it far more difficult for rescuers to get to the beleaguered city, and for refugees to leave. You will never guess who built, operated, and maintained these facilities. Yes, it was government!

It of course cannot be denied that various oil drilling rigs also came unglued, and that these were all private enterprises. One of them even collided with a bridge, greatly damaging it. However, there is a significant difference between the two types of events. The market test of profit and loss applies only to the latter, not to the former. Those oil companies that built their platforms more strongly will tend to grab market share from those that did not. No such regimen operates in the governmental sector. Imagine if the oil drilling rigs were all built by the state. They would have undoubtedly created far more damage.

II. The Dead Hand of the Past

It is by no means clear that there should even *be* a city in the territory now occupied by New Orleans.

Ideally, under a regime of economic freedom, what determines whether a geographical area should be settled at all, and if so how intensively? It depends upon whether or not, in the eyes of the human economic actors involved, the subjective costs outweigh the benefits. The reason no one lives in the north or south poles, and that population density in Siberia, Northern Canada, and the desert areas of Nevada is very low, is that the disadvantages are vastly greater than the advantages in those places.

However, if government subsidizes building in areas people on their own would not choose to locate, then the populace can no longer allocate itself geographically in a rational manner. Similarly, the government declares drought-stricken farmlands an emergency area, and heavily subsidizes agriculture in such locales, there is also misallocation of settlement in this regard.

The Federal Emergency Management Agency (FEMA), created in 1979, became part of the U.S. Department of Homeland Security only on March 1, 2003. The federal government has been doling out gobs of money to inhabitants of areas struck by tornados, storms, snow, and other inclement weather for years. Such declarations number in the dozens for 2005 alone. Southern Louisiana, Mississippi, and Alabama have already been declared federal disaster areas. Tons of money will pour into these political jurisdictions. Thus, locational decisions are and will continue to be rendered less rational than otherwise, if people had to pay the full costs of their geographical settlement decisions.

It may well be that with the advantage of hindsight, the Big Easy is like several of these other places: not too cold, or drought-stricken, but too low, below sea level, and thus too much in danger of being flooded.

Mises in *Epistemological Problems of Economics* states this regard:

> Suppose that, making use of our entire store of technological skill and our present-day knowledge of geography, we were to undertake to resettle the earth's surface in such a way that we should afterwards be in a position to take maximum advantage of the natural distribution of raw materials. And suppose further that for this purpose the entire capital wealth of the present were at our disposal in a form that would allow us to invest it in whatever way was regarded as the most suitable for the end in view.
>
> In such a case the world would certainly take on an appearance that would be very considerably different from the one it now presents. Many areas would be less densely populated. ... The great trade routes would follow other courses.

At first glance, this does not support a New Orleans with anything like its close-to-one-half-million population at its present location. Yes, this city is situated at the mouth of a great river, and offers a world-class port to international shipping. On the other hand as recent events have so tragically demonstrated, these benefits may be more than offset by the fact that it lies below sea level.

Does this mean that New Orleans would be doomed under a free enterprise system? This is quite possibly the case, if we could do everything all over again, and start *de novo*, at the present time. But not necessarily, given that vast investment has already been made in streets, buildings, pipes, etc. Even though, perhaps, if we knew then what we know now, no city would have been erected south of Lake Ponchartrain, it does not logically follow that it should not be rebuilt at present, under realistic assumptions.

Given that New Orleans is now located where it is, it is entirely possible that it is economical for there to remain a large human settlement in that area. What cannot be denied is that when government enters the picture, economic calculation of this sort becomes impossible.

Mises continues his analysis:

> With regard to choice of location ... new plants appear most efficient in the light of the existing situation. But ... consideration for capital goods produced in the past under certain circumstances makes the technologically best ... (location) ... appear uneconomical. History and the past have their say. An economic calculation that did not take them into account would be deficient. We are not only of today; we are heirs of the past as well. Our capital wealth is handed down from the past, and this fact has its consequences. ... [S]trict rationality ... induces the entrepreneur to continue production in a disadvantageous location ...

That is, New Orleans might well be a "disadvantageous location" based on the assumption that we can with hindsight rearrange all previous locational decisions. But, we can do no such thing. Rather, capital (buildings, roads, pipelines, etc.) are bequeathed to us *at a certain location*. As it happens, lots of valuable capital is located in New Orleans. This fact would incline us to reinvest in that locale, storms be damned. But only private enterprise can make such a decision on a rational basis. When government muddies the waters, this cannot take place.

The best way then, to rationally determine whether or not the Big Easy should be saved, is to leave this decision entirely to free enterprise — to capitalist entrepreneurs, who, alone, can rationally make such determinations. As the Austrian side of the socialist calculation debate has demonstrated, only with market prices can this be done. Moreover, private owners make such decisions with their own money, or funds entrusted to them;

if they err, they alone suffer. They do not bring the rest of us down along with them.

III. WEATHER SOCIALISM

But there is a third element we cannot ignore: weather socialism.

According to an old adage, critics of government can properly blame this institution for many things, but bad weather is not among them. Wrong, wrong. At the risk of sounding out of step with the mainstream (a new experience for me) the state is responsible not only for hurricanes, but for tornados, storms, typhoon, tsunami, excessive heat, excessive cold, too much rain, too little rain, floods, droughts, desertification, tempests, squalls, gales, rainstorms, snowstorms, thunderstorms, blizzards, downpours, cyclones, whirlwinds, twisters, monsoons, torrential rains, cloudbursts, showers, etc. You name any kind of bad weather conditions, and the government is to blame.

Why, pray tell? Because the state at all levels grabs off almost 50 percent of the GDP in taxes, and its regulations account for a significant additional amount of wealth not created. If the voracious government left all or even most of the property created by its rightful owners — those who created it in the first place with their own hands — the weather problem could undoubtedly be better addressed by private enterprise.

And for what wondrous tasks does the government waste trillions of our earnings? Let me count some few of the ways. It subsidizes farmers who ought to be allowed to go bankrupt when they cannot earn an honest profit in their industry. As the number of farmers has declined over the years, the number of bureaucrats in the Department of Agriculture has increased. Welfare for farmers and agricultural mandarins.

Speaking of welfare, this is but the tip of the iceberg. Our masters in Washington, D.C. distribute our hard-earned money to people who bear children they cannot afford to feed, and to corporate welfare bums. Then there is the Department of Education (weren't the Republicans going to get rid of this sore on the body politic?) that presides over a public school system that warehouses and mis-educates our children.

And don't get me started on our system of medical socialism that wastes yet other precious resources. We don't have HillaryCare yet but we are well on our way. Then, too, we must count government throwing our money at the post office, the space program, ethanol, foreign "aid," unemployment insurance, the list goes on and on.

The drug war incarcerates thousands of innocent people — who could be out there creating additional wealth — at a cost exceeding tuition and room and board at some of our most prestigious universities. Last but certainly not least, speaking of war, the U.S. has been bullying its way around the world for decades, creating untold havoc. Katrina can't hold a candle to our armed forces in terms of killing innocent people. There are no truer words than that "War is the health of the State."

Suppose that the "public sector" were not wasting untold riches. What has this got to do with improving weather conditions? Well, a lot of the money returned to the long-suffering taxpayers (and much of the additional wealth created by the ending of economic regulations) would be allocated in the usual directions: sailboats and pianos, and violin lessons and better food, and more entertainment, etc. But some of it would likely be invested in more research and development as to the causes and cures of unwelcome weather conditions.

Is there any doubt that in 100, or 1,000, or 10,000 years — assuming the government does not blow us all up before then — we will no longer be plagued by uncooperative clouds? I don't say that if the state disappeared tomorrow the next day we would have clear weather (and rain to order from 2 a.m. – 4 a.m.), but surely the ending of the former would bring about the latter that much more quickly.

How would this work? Wouldn't the problem of "public goods" rend the market a "failure," as our friends from the Chicago so-called "free enterprise" school of economics would have it? Their argument is that if I come up with a way to stop storms dead in their tracks, or better yet, orchestrate matters such that they do not form in the first place, everyone else will "free ride" on my innovation. The other beneficiaries will simply refuse to pay me for this boon I confer on them, so I will not invest any money on this task in the first place. And neither will you. So the private enterprise system cannot handle such challenges.

Stuff and nonsense.

First of all, this task need not be accomplished on a for-profit basis. Non-profit organizations, too, are part of the private sector of the economy. Just looking at the charitable outpourings to New Orleanians from all corners of the country, we can see that there is no shortage of benevolence and good will for the victims of Katrina. I should single out for special mention in this regard that "evil" profit maximizing large corporation that grinds down suppliers, immiserates its own workers due to its anti-union policies, bankrupts small grocers, and just all around exploits everything else it touches. This hated corporation contributed $1 million to the Salvation Army for hurricane relief. More recently, Wal-Mart committed an additional $15 million for this purpose. As part of this commitment, Wal-Mart will "establish mini-Wal-Mart stores in areas impacted by the hurricane. Items such as clothing, diapers, baby wipes, food, formula, toothbrushes, bedding, and water will be given out free of charge to those with a demonstrated need."

In contrast, I do not recommend the American Red Cross. I still have not forgiven them for turning aside risks of spreading AIDS and infecting hundreds of people, many of them hemophiliacs. Unhappily, from my own point of view, Wal-Mart, sent another $1 million to the Red Cross. But if you want to really help the inhabitants of the Gulf Coast long term, support organizations that unveil government misdeeds and the state libertarian parties of Louisiana, Mississippi, or Alabama. But not the national party, until they deal with this issue.

The point is, if we the people had vastly more money at our disposal than we do now, thanks to government profligacy with our funds, we would be able to donate some of it to the not-for-profit sector to engage in research and development for weather control.

Second, the market has a way of internalizing the so-called externalities that supposedly prevent firms from providing storm-busting services. Within limits, and depending upon technology, the purveyors of flood insurance would be able to turn the rain and wind on and off like a spigot, depending upon the locational densities of their clientele.

For example, if in area A 90 percent of the landowners are members of Hurricane Busters, Inc., and in area B only 10 percent are, there is little doubt as to which will be better served by this particular firm. Then, too, there will be not only social pressure, but economic pressure, for large firms in any geographical area to sign up for such services. Those that do not (particularly in states stretching from Texas to Florida, and most certainly in New Orleans) will tend to find their customer base disappearing.

As but one small instance of this phenomenon, companies with large parking lots have recently instituted reserved spaces for pregnant women and new moms. No government agency forced them to do any such thing. (Prediction: the state will soon do just that, so as to garner credit for this very humane and profitable policy.) As this movement catches on, few will be able to resist. A similar situation is likely to arise with regard to protection from hurricanes. At the very least, if government would but get out of the way, it would clear the path for private enterprise to more quickly bring us to the day when the Katrinas of the future will be obviated.

To conclude, here is what I see as the libertarian position on the storm and its aftermath. No national guard or other representatives of the state should be brought in. They are in effect "murderers and thieves." Instead, private police agencies, appointed by property owners, should deal with the looters.

Further, no tax money should be poured into New Orleans. These are stolen funds, and should be returned to their rightful owners, the taxpayers of the nation. Of course, this applies, in spades, to those victimized by Katrina. But the refunds should be in the form of money, not expenditures for rebuilding, which their proper owners may or may not favor.

Private enterprise alone should determine if the Big Easy is worth saving or not. Problems of "transactions costs" will be far easier to overcome than challenges presented by an inept and economically irrational government. Possibly a Donald Trump type might try to buy up all the buildings at a fraction of their previous value, and save his new investment by levee building and water pumping. He wouldn't need to get 100 percent sales. A lesser amount, say, 90 percent, might do, and he would only make his initial purchases subject to reaching this level. That is, he might first purchase options to buy.

CHAPTER 18

Clean, Cool Private Water: Government Water Means Trouble*

T wo tragedies have recently occurred in Canada, one which has been given much publicity, the other only a little. As the wrong lessons have been drawn from both, we do well to reconsider each case, and to more carefully consider what they portend.

One calamity occurred in Walkerton, Ontario, where an outbreak of E. coli bacteria eventuated in the deaths of seven residents and the sickening of thousands of others. The Conservative government of Premier Mike Harris was widely blamed for this episode, since it had previously contracted out to private sources responsibility for drinking water in the province.

The second disaster took place at an artificial lake at Birds Hill Provincial Park in Winnipeg, Manitoba. This was the drowning of 18-year-old Katarzyna Zarzecki, who died while swimming and was unable to be rescued by the beach patrol. This comes hard on the heels of the drowning deaths of two small boys at the same facility during the summer of 2000.

As with the Walkerton cases, these deaths were also widely blamed upon privatization by the leftist media, because the life guarding responsibilities at this lake were also contracted out by provincial authorities to a for-profit corporation.

My claim is that these tragedies in Ontario and Manitoba occurred not because of these privatizations, but in spite of them; that the lesson to

---

*August 3, 2001.

be learned from both episodes, paradoxically, is not that we need less involvement with the free enterprise system, but more. I say "paradoxically"
because in the minds of most people, particularly the journalists who have
written about these two stories, the case seems very straightforward: at one
time these facilities were both under the control of the government, and
all was well. Then there came a time when each was privatized, whereupon difficulties broke out. The lesson seems obvious: re-provincialize both
amenities, and while we are at it, nationalize pretty much everything else,
because if the government is more efficient than the private sector, why
should we have much of the latter in any case?

Does anyone see a difficulty here? What passes for "common sense"
amongst the Canadian chattering classes has been tried elsewhere, and
found wanting. Very wanting. Now, let's see, where was that? Oh, yes, now
I remember: it was the Soviet Union and its satellite countries, which all
went belly up, economically speaking, late in the last century. And now we
are seriously considering a "made in Canada policy" of nationalization that
is a pale carbon-copy emulation of the failure of communism? For shame!

But it is not enough to know that greater reliance on the public sector
will fail; if we are to eradicate this sort of thinking we must know why as
well. Otherwise, people will continue to think that what happened to the
USSR was an accident, and that "it can't happen here."

So why is it that markets typically outperform governments in providing services such as paper clips and corn and wrist watches and milk, and
also water quality and life guarding at beaches? It is due to the profit motive
and competition. If the pizza in my restaurant is lousy, you go elsewhere.
If you do, I am given a strong market signal to mend the error of my ways,
and if I cannot, to get into a line of work where I can make a contribution to society. Contrast this to Pizza Canada, based on the same economic
principles that have long endeared us to Canada Post. Here, if you don't like
the food product, you can go elsewhere, but Pizza Canada keeps on going
and going, just like the energizer bunny, courtesy of tax payments mulcted
from consumers unwilling to give this operation their dollar votes.

For some reason, there is a fetish in Canada about water. Yes, other
things may be safely left to the market, but not this fluid. Water is special.
Nonsense on stilts! H_2O is just another liquid. Free enterprise supplies us
with high quality milk, soda pop, beer, wine, liquor, fruit juice, and every
other liquid under the sun. Why should water be any different?

It might be objected that the quality of these other substances is controlled by the state apparatus; but the same could apply to water. In any

case, which do you trust more: a government monopoly bureaucratic certification agency, or a competitive industry dedicated to these same ends? Realize that the same weeding-out process that applies to pizza also encompasses quality assurance. Thalidomide for morning sickness, after all, was approved by a government agency that by its very nature could never go bankrupt. We ought to more greatly appreciate the profit and loss system that automatically encourages success and penalizes failure. The Soviets, lacking this feedback mechanism, fell victim to economic arteriosclerosis. We do not get good burgers from McDonalds, high quality pizza, pure beverages from Coca Cola, wonderful cars from Rolls Royce, because of government oversight, which is subject to bribes in any case. No, these things come to us, and also Kosher foods another private institution of quality control, from the market sector.

Yes, private enterprise is not perfect. There will be injuries and even deaths in areas under its control. A few people drown, and others drink impure water. More would suffer these fates under bureaucratic management. Consider the some 3,000 Canadian motorists and pedestrians who lose their lives each year in traffic accidents on roads owned and managed by various governmental jurisdictions (the number is roughly ten-fold this in the U.S.). Why is there no hue and cry to privatize these properties? Could it be that due to the fact that under the veneer of appreciation for capitalism there is still a strong subterranean yearning for the Communist way of life?

D. Labor Economics

CHAPTER 19

The Evil of Unions; In the Public As Well As the Private Sector[*]

According to our friends on the left, the reason we need unions is because without them, employers would grind employees into the ground. Were organized labor to disappear, wages would plummet; workers would have to work on Sundays ("If you don't come in Sunday, don't bother coming in Monday"), tip their hat to their bosses, and suffer all sorts of other indignities, including losing virtually all improvements in working conditions made over the last century.

Of course, this is all wrong. Wages and working conditions are not set by firms. Rather, they depend upon the productivity of labor, more technically on the marginal revenue product of the worker. This can be defined as the extra amount of revenue brought in by adding one more person to the payroll. For example, if there were 1,000 workers creating an item that sold for $x, and then the 1,001st employee came on board and the firms sales rose to $x + $7, then the marginal revenue productivity of the last person hired would be $7 per hour.

Wages cannot long be higher than this amount, or the company will lose money on every worker it hires. For example, if compensation is $10, and revenue taken in due to the efforts of the worker is $7, then the firm loses $3 every hour the man is on the shop floor.

---

[*]September 14, 2005.

On the other hand, a situation cannot endure where wages are lower than this amount. For example, suppose pay was $2 per hour, while productivity remained at the $7 level we are considering. Then, the employer would earn a pure profit of $5 every hour. This cannot last for two reasons. First, other companies would have incentive to hire such a worker away from his employer. Assuming that the productivity of the latter would be the same $7 on the premises of any member of the industry, a competitor could offer, say, $2.25. This would be a substantial increase over and above the present salary of $2, and yet would allow the newcomer to earn a profit of $7 minus $2.25 = $4.75. But if this would work, so would a bid of $2.50, $2.75, $3.00, etc. Where would this process end? As near to $7 as allowed by the costs of finding such "underpaid" workers and convincing them to switch jobs for higher pay. Second, workers talk to each other. An employee worth $7 but paid less than that would be tempted to quit if he found out that his associates at other stores or factories were earning more. Thus, wages for workers of this skill level will tend to earn $7. This does not mean that under free enterprise there will be no deviations from this amount. There will be. The market is continually changing. But there is an inexorable tendency for wages to continually move in the direction of this equilibration.

If wages were really set by employers, why is it that employees such as Shaquille O'Neal, Brad Pitt, Brittney Spears, and Bill Gates all earn mega bucks? Generosity? No, the reason they do is because their productivity (ability to fill seats in sports arenas, movie theaters, concert halls in the case of the first three, and manage a large company for the latter) is very, very high. If their present employers did not pay them satisfactorily (that is, in accordance with productivity) others would gladly jump in and do so.

When unions artificially boost wages above this stipulated $7 productivity, they look good in the short run. But in the long run they create business failures and rust belts. Just as you cannot shove the water in the bathtub in a downward direction without slopping some of it out onto the floor, it is impossible for any substantial length of time to maintain wages above productivity levels. (Actually, the former is a mere physical impossibility; the latter, in addition, violates the economic laws of logic, or praxeology.)

What determines the level of productivity, and hence the wages that are dependent upon it? This is based on how hard and how smart people work, and the amount and sophistication of the tools and capital equipment they are given by their employer to work with. This, in turn, depends upon how much saving occurred in the previous periods, and, even before that, how economically free and law abiding is the populace. The more reliance on private property rights and free enterprise, other things equal, the better in this regard.

If organized labor is really the only institution that stands between the workingman and abject poverty, how is it that real wages have been increasing, while the rate of unionization has been declining over the last half century (see Table 1)? Why is it the some industries that have never come within a million miles of unions (computers, banking, accounting) pay very high wages, often in excess of that earned by the rank and file? Given that they are at the mercy of the capitalist pigs, should they not have been ground into the dust? How can it be that the south, which is the least unionized part of the country, is the fastest growing? What accounts for the fact that countries where western style unionism is all but unknown (Hong Kong, Singapore, Japan) are economic powerhouses, with standards of living envied in many places on the globe?

Be this as it may, it is all dismissed by professors, pundits and politicians on the left side of the aisle. Let it never be said that the present writer has no empathy for these sorts of people. In order to demonstrate this, I shall now assume, *arguendo*, that everything the opponents of free enterprise say about the employer's relationship with the employee is true. The former is a blood-sucker, always ready to pounce on the hapless worker. The bosses have cash registers for hearts, and dollar signs on their eyes; no pity for the downtrodden masses ever bestirs them. Had they their way, the situation of the worker would be hopeless indeed.

As part of this present touchy-feely analysis of mine, I must also acknowledge the benevolent role played by the government in labor relations. Were it not for magnificent pro-organized labor legislation such as the Clayton Act, the Railway Labor Act, the Davis-Bacon Act, the Norris-LaGuardia Act, National Industry Recovery Act, the Wagner Act, the National Labor Relations Board Act, the Byrnes Anti-Strikebreaker Law, the Walsh-Healy Act ,and Fair Labor Standards Act, the firm would not have been taken down a peg or two, and the workers plight would have been horrific.

Okay, okay, enough with the economic illiteracy. Instead, let me ask proponents of these sentiments just one single solitary question: if the government is such a great institution, that totally eschews profiting from the blood, sweat, and toil of the workingman, from whence comes the justification of, wait for it, public sector unions? My point here is that these sorts of labor organizations are simply incompatible with the leftist case (articulated

Table 1

U.S. Union Membership, 1948–2004
(numbers in the thousands)

Year	Percent Workforce	Total Members	Year	Percent Workforce	Total Members
1948	31.8	14,271	1977	26.2	21,632
1949	31.9	13,935	1978	25.1	21,756
1950	31.6	14,294	1979	24.5	22,025
1951	31.7	15,139	1980	23.2	20,968
1952	32.0	15,632	1981	22.6	20,646
1953	32.5	16,310	1982	21.9	19,571
1954	32.3	15,808	1983	20.7	18,633
1955	31.8	16,126	1984	18.8	17,340
1956	31.4	16,446	1985	18.0	16,996
1957	30.2	16,497	1986	17.5	16,975
1958	30.3	15,570	1987	17.0	16,913
1959	29.0	15,438	1988	16.8	17,002
1960	28.6	15,516	1989	16.4	16,960
1961	28.5	15,400	1990	16.1	16,740
1962	30.4	16,893	1991	16.1	16,568
1963	30.2	17,133	1992	15.8	16,390
1964	30.2	17,597	1993	15.8	16,598
1965	30.1	18,268	1994	15.5	16,748
1966	29.6	18,922	1995	14.9	16,326
1967	29.9	19,667	1996	14.5	16,269
1968	29.5	20,017	1997	14.1	16,110
1969	28.7	20,185	1998	13.9	16,211
1970	29.6	20,990	1999	13.9	16,477
1971	29.1	20,711	2000	13.5	16,258
1972	28.8	21,205	2001	13.5	16,275
1973	28.5	21,881	2002	13.3	16,146
1974	28.3	22,165	2003	12.9	15,776
1975	28.9	22,207	2004	12.5	15,472
1976	27.9	22,153			

Source: http://www.laborresearch.org/charts.php?id=29

above) to the effect that the capitalist is an exploiter, and that the government has rescued the worker from the baleful influence of the corporation. If the state is so wonderful as all that, why the need for a public sector union, all of whose members have the benevolent government as their boss?

Look at Table 2. As can be clearly seen, if present trends long continue, private sector unions will all but disappear. The only thing propping up over all union membership percentages are those organized against the government. Organized against the government? That wonderful institution that protects the working stiff from the evil capitalists? The one responsible for the plethora of pro-union legislation mentioned above? This can only make sense to those entirely innocent not only of elementary economic reasoning, but of basic logic as well. It is time, it is long past time, for all public sector unions to be disbanded.

TABLE 2

PERCENTAGE OF THE LABOR FORCE THAT IS UNIONIZED

YEAR	PUBLIC	PRIVATE	TOTAL
2004	36.4	7.9	12.5
2003	37.2	8.2	12.9
2002	37.5	8.5	13.3
2001	37.4	9.0	13.5
2000	37.5	9.0	13.5
1999	37.3	9.4	13.9
1998	37.5	9.5	13.9
1997	37.2	9.8	14.1
1996	27.7	10.2	14.5
1995	37.5	10.4	14.9
1994	38.7	10.9	15.5
1993	37.7	11.2	15.8
1992	36.7	–	15.8

Sources:
- http://www.bls.gov/opub/ted/2002/jan/wk3/art03.htm
- http://www.bls.gov/news.release/union2.nr0.htm
- http://www.bls.gov/cps/wlf-table38-2005.pdf
- ftp://ftp.bls.gov/pub/news.release/History/union2.013197.news
- http://www.bls.gov/schedule/archives/all_nr.htm#UNION2

Or is it?

Let us turn to one last issue in conclusion. When a public sector union (firemen, garbage men, post office workers, librarians, teachers, bus drivers, civil servants, etc.) goes on strike, whom does the libertarian favor? They are in effect both of them criminal gangs, only one is usually far stronger than the other. One stance is, at any given time, root for the weakest one. That virtually always implies the public sector union. Of course, this means to the extent the rooting is effective, higher wages, and ultimately an increase in taxes will result. This can be obviated when the government bears down and does not accede to the wishes of these labor organizations, but the downside is that the state, the source of union power in the first place, emerges even stronger. Perhaps the best reaction is "A pox on both your houses." In which case it is clear that we libertarians should champion an end to public sector unions.

But what is crystal clear is that the existence of these labor organizations cannot be reconciled with the usual leftist rhetoric about mean-spirited private capitalists and benevolent politicians. Were this the case socialists would defend private unions only. However, they of course do not. This is yet one more bit of evidence attesting to their irrationality.

CHAPTER 20

Is There a Right To Unionize?
It All Depends*

I resist the notion that we have a "right to unionize" or that unionization is akin, or, worse, an implication of, the right to freely associate. Yes, theoretically, a labor organization *could* limit itself to organizing a mass quit unless they got what they wanted. That would indeed be an implication of the law of free association.

But every union with which I am familiar reserves the right to employ violence (that is, to initiate violence) against competing workers, e.g., scabs, whether in a "blue collar way" by beating them up, or in a "white collar way" by getting laws passed compelling employers to deal with them, and not with the scabs. (Does anyone know of a counter example to this? If you know of any, I'd be glad to hear of it. I once thought I had found one: the Christian Labor Association of Canada. But based on an interview with them I can say that while they eschew "blue collar" aggression, they support the "white collar" version.)

But what of the fact that there are many counterexamples: unions that have not actually engaged in the initiation of violence? Moreover, there are even people associated for many years with organized labor who have never witnessed the outbreak of actual violence.

Let me clarify my position. My opposition is not merely to violence, but, rather, to "violence, *or* the threat of violence." My position is that, often, no

---

*January 1, 2004.

actual violence is needed, if the threat is serious enough, which, I contend, always obtains under unionism, at least as practiced in the U.S. and Canada.

Probably, the IRS never engaged in the actual use of physical violence in its entire history. (It is mostly composed of nerds, not physically aggressive people.) This is because it relies on the courts-police of the U.S. government who have overwhelming power. But it would be superficial to contend that the IRS does not engage in "violence, or the threat of violence." This holds true also for the state trooper who stops you and gives you a ticket. They are, and are trained to be, exceedingly polite. Yet, "violence, or the threat of violence" permeates their entire relationship with you.

I do not deny, moreover, that sometimes, management also engages in "violence, or the threat of violence." My only contention is that it is possible to point to numerous cases where they do not, while the same is impossible for organized labor, at least in the countries I am discussing.

In my view, the threat emanating from unions is objective, not subjective. It is the threat, in the old blue collar days, that any competing worker, a "scab," would be beat up if he tried to cross a picket line, and, in the modern white collar days, that any employer who fires a striking employee union member and substitutes for him a replacement worker as a permanent hire, will be found in violation of various labor laws. (Why, by the way, is it not "discriminatory," and "hateful," to describe workers willing to take less pay, and to compete with unionized labor, as "scabs"? Should not this be considered on a par with using the "N" word for blacks, or the "K" word for Jews?)

Suppose a small scrawny hold-up man confronts a big burly football-player-type guy and demands his money, threatening that if the big guy does not give it up, the little guy will kick his butt. I call this an objective threat, and I don't care if the big guy laughs himself silly in reaction. Second scenario. Same as the first, only this time the little guy whips out a pistol, and threatens to shoot the big guy unless he hands over his money.

Now, there are two kinds of big guys. One will feel threatened, and hand over his money. The second will attack the little guy (in self-defense, I contend). Perhaps he is feeling omnipotent. Perhaps he is wearing a bullet-proof vest. It does not matter. The threat is a threat is a threat, regardless of the reaction of the big guy, regardless of his inner psychological response.

Now let us return to labor management relations. The union objectively threatens scabs, and employers who hire them. This, nowadays, is purely a matter of law, not psychological feelings on anyone's part. In contrast, while it cannot be denied that sometimes employers initiate violence against workers, they need not *necessarily* do it, qua employer. (Often, however, such violence is in self-defense.)

This is similar to the point I made about the pimp in my book *Defending the Undefendable*: For this purpose, I don't care if each and every pimp has in fact initiated violence. Nor does it matter if they do it every hour on the hour. This is not a *necessary* characteristic of being a pimp. Even if there are no non-violent pimps in existence, we can still *imagine* one such. Even if all employers always initiated violence against employees, still, we can imagine employers who do not. In very sharp contrast indeed, because of labor legislation they all support, we cannot even imagine unionized labor that does not threaten the initiation of violence.

Murray N. Rothbard was bitterly opposed to unions. This emanated from two sources. First, as a libertarian theoretician, because organized labor necessarily threatens violence (see *Man, Economy and State*). Second, based on personal harm suffered at their hands by his family (see Justin Raimondo, *An Enemy of the State: The Life of Murray N. Rothbard*).

We must never succumb to the siren song of union thuggery.

CHAPTER 21

In Defense of Scabs; The Limited Justification for Trade Unions*

I wrote a piece called "Is There a Right to Unionize?" (see chapter 20) and received dozens and dozens of responses. Many of them raised interesting points I did not address in that article, or, at least, not fully enough. Rather than responding to all these letters, substantively and in detail, I thought I would reply to some of the points in a second essay.

1. Unionism Is Legitimate

Many insisted that theoretically, unions are compatible with the free society. I agree, I agree. Nothing I said before should be taken to be inconsistent with this view. All such a union would have to do is to eschew both white- and blue-collar crime. I only argue that it has never happened in fact, not that it would be impossible for it to occur.

However, I am something of a fuss-pot about language. Surely, a workers' association that totally eschews the initiation of violence, or even the threat thereof, deserves different nomenclature from organizations it only superficially resembles; e.g., unions. My suggestion is that we not characterize as a union any labor organization that strictly limits itself to the threat of quitting en masse.

---

*January 5, 2004.

What, then, should we call a group of workers who eschew both beating up "scabs" and laws compelling employers to bargain with them? Here are some possibilities: workers' associations, employees' groups, organizations of staff members, etc.

Thus. Are workers' associations as defined above compatible with free enterprise? You bet your boots they are. Do unions, or organized labor qualify in this regard? No, a thousand times no.

2. Public Sector Unions

One reader, a very distinguished fellow columnist, takes the position that public sector unions are the worst of them all (not his exact language, which is too pithy to be fully recorded here).

In my view, public sector unions present theoretical libertarianism with a very complex challenge (albeit in a slightly different manner than do private sector unions: in this case, they are not necessarily incompatible with the free society, but, as it happens, there are no actual cases in existence of such employee organizations that *are* consistent with economic freedom).

The complexity presented by public sector unions is that, on the one hand, from a libertarian perspective they can be seen as a counterweight to illegitimate governments, while on the other hand they constitute an attack on innocent citizens. Each of these different roles calls for a somewhat different libertarian response.

Let us take the first case first. For the limited government libertarian, or minarchist, the state is illegitimate if, and to the extent it exceeds its proper bounds. These, typically, include armies (for *defense* against foreign powers, not *offense* against them), police to keep local criminals in check (that is, rapists and murderers, etc., not victimless "criminals" such as drug dealers, prostitutes, etc.), and courts to determine guilt or innocence. Some more moderate advocates of laissez faire add to this list roads, communicable disease inoculations, fire protection and mosquito control. For the anarcho-libertarian, of course, there is no such thing as a licit government.

What, then, are libertarians to say about a public sector teachers' union, on strike against a state school? (A similar analysis holds for public sector unions in garbage collection, post office, buses, or in any other industry where government involvement is improper in the first place). It is my contention that the correct analysis of this situation is, "A plague on both your houses." For not one, but *both* of these organizations is illegitimate. There is no libertarian who can favor government schools, whether anarchist or minarchist (Milton Friedman, who champions public schools, as long as they operate under a voucher system, thus falls outside the realm of libertarianism on this question.) So, on one side of this dispute, there is illegitimacy. But the same applies to the other, the union side, as we have previously demonstrated. Thus, there are here two contending forces, both of them in the wrong. From a *strategic* point of view, we may well even support the union vis-à-vis the government, since they are the weaker of the two opponents. But from a principled perspective, my main interest here, we must look upon the two of them as would all men of good will witness a battle between the Blood and the Crips, or between Nazi Germany and Communist U.S.S.R. Root for both of them!

Now, let us consider the second case. Here, we note that the public sector union does much more than attack illegitimate government. It also vastly inconveniences practically the entire populace. When schools are closed, garbage is not collected, the buses do not run — because public sector unions utilize violence and the threat thereof to these ends — then the libertarian response is clear: opposition, root and branch.

Let us take one last crack at public sector unions, which brings about a further complication. One of my correspondents mentions that "The last 2003 show of ABC's *20/20* news show had a story on how public employee unions are fighting against people who volunteer for the public good," referring to "one of the great *Give Me a Break* segments by host John Stossel" (see on this "No Good Deed Goes Unpunished: Are Volunteers Taking Workers' Jobs?" ABCNEWS.com).

The general issue is that citizens have been volunteering to do things like help public sector unionists collect trash in parks, aid them in planting flowers, help them stack books in public libraries, etc., and the unions have reacted viciously, as is their wont.

Before we can shed libertarian light on this contentious issue, let us first ask, What is the libertarian analysis of ordinary people volunteering to help the government do jobs it should not be doing in the first place? To put it in this way is almost to answer the question.

There is no difference in principle between volunteering to help the state perform illegitimate acts (of course, these are not illicit, per se, as are concentration camps; rather, it is improper, in libertarian theory, for *governments* to take on such responsibilities) such as regarding libraries, schools, parks, etc., and sending them monetary donations for such purposes. In either case, one is aiding and abetting evil, and risking being found guilty of crimes against humanity by a future libertarian Nuremberg trial court.

Repeat after me: free enterprise, good, (excessive) government, bad. Once again from the top: *free enterprise, good, (excessive) government, bad!* The appellation, "libertarian," is an honorific. It is too precious to be bestowed on all those who claim it. It is my contention that people who support (excessive) government are simply not entitled to its use. (At least in the specific context in which they violate the non-aggression axiom. John Stossel is indeed a libertarian on many other issues, but certainly not on this one.)

Here is a lesson for libertarians. If you want to be worthy of this designation, and desire to contribute money to a good cause, do not give to a government that goes beyond its legitimate authority. There are many worthy causes that *oppose* statist depredations, *not* support them. If you want to be worthy of this honorific, and wish to donate time to a good cause, e.g., by collecting garbage, planting flowers, or filing books, etc., then do so for the relevant *private* groups, whether charitable or profit seeking, it matters not one whit.

3. CAN A LIBERTARIAN JOIN A UNION?

Several asked if it is proper, if it is even logically possible, for a libertarian to join a coercive union? Much as I hate to be controversial (okay, okay, I don't mind it a bit) my answer is Yes. There are many issues upon which I disagree with William F. Buckley, but his decision to join ACTRA is not one of them. (This was the requirement imposed upon him for being allowed to air his television show, *Firing Line*.)

Why would I take such a seemingly perverted stance? Let me answer by indirection. Given that it is illegitimate for the government to run schools and universities, is it illegitimate for a libertarian to join them whether as a student or a professor? Given that it is illegitimate for the government to organize a post office, is it illegitimate for a libertarian to mail a letter? Given that it is illegitimate for the government to build and manage roads, streets and sidewalks, is it illegitimate for a libertarian to utilize these amenities?

True confession time. I have been a student at public schools; grade school, high school, and college. I have even been a professor at several public colleges and universities. I regularly purchase stamps from the evil government post office, and mail letters. I walk on public sidewalks, and avail myself of streets and highways. Mea culpa? Not a bit of it.

If Ayn Rand's heroic character Ragnar Danneskjöld has taught us anything, it is that the government is not the legitimate owner of what it claims. Why, then, should we respect its "private property rights" when there is no practical reason to do so? If this means that libertarians can partake of services for which they favor privatization, then so be it.

Similarly, with coercive unions. If a hold-up man demands your money at the point of a gun, giving it up is *not* incompatible with libertarianism, even though it amounts to acquiescing in theft. If organized labor threatens you with bodily harm unless you join with it and pay dues to it, I cannot think that agreeing to do so per se removes the victim from the ranks of libertarianism. Buckley, to give him credit, never ceased inveighing against the injustice done to him in this way. If he had reversed field, and starting *defending* unions, then what little claim he has to be a libertarian would have vanished. In this regard, there is all the world of difference between a Marxist professor at a public university who promotes interventionism, and a libertarian who opposes it.

4. Not Aware of Violence

Several objected on the grounds that they were not aware of any violence in their own unions. But, many employees of the IRS are probably not aware that what they are doing amounts to the threat of the initiation of violence. I don't see why all union members should necessarily be aware of this for my thesis (this is hardly original with me) to be correct. My understanding is that after the British left India, the government of the latter began polling people in far removed rural villages as to their thoughts on this matter; they had to stop when they learned that they were not aware that the British had even arrived there in the first place. Heck, there are probably some people out there who still think the earth is flat, or that socialism is an ethical and efficacious system! That does not make it so.

5. Self-defense

Some readers objected on the grounds that union violence did indeed exist, but was justified on the grounds that this was only in self-defense, against employers, scabs, or foreigners. Let us consider each of these in turn.

Yes, employers are violent too. The Pinkertons spring immediately to mind in this regard. Some of these cases were justified in self-defense, against prior union aggression, some were not. In the former case, there is certainly no warrant for invasive behavior on the part of organized labor.

But even the latter cases cannot serve as justification for pervasive union aggression, even against non-invading employers. (It is only a Marxist who would claim that employers are necessarily offensive; for an exposure of this fallacy, see Eugen Böhm-Bawerk, *Capital and Interest*, particularly his "Exploitation Theory of Socialism-Communism.") At best, this can validate self-defense on the part of the rank and file in those cases of employer aggression only.

And what of "scabs?" The claim, here, is that "scabs" are stealing, or, better yet, attempting to steal, union jobs. But the scab can only "steal" a job if it is *owned*, like a coat, or a car. However, a job is very different. It is *not* something anyone can own. Rather, a job is an *agreement* between two parties, employer and employee. But when an employer is trying to hire a scab and fire the unionist, this shows he no longer *agrees*. Do not be fooled by the expression "my job." It does not denote ownership, any more than "my wife," "my husband," "my friend," "my customer," or "my tailor" indicates possession in any of those contexts. Rather, all of these phrases are indicative of voluntary interaction, and end (apart from marriage laws which may prohibit this) when the agreement ceases.

Then, there is the supposed "threat" imposed by Mexican workers (or Indian or Japanese workers, whoever is the economic Hitler of the day). Remember that "giant sucking sound?" The best remedy for this bit of economic illiteracy is to read up on free trade. Henry Hazlitt's book, *Economics in One Lesson*, would be a great place to start.

6. But They Signed a Contract

Several respondents argued that since the employer signed a labor contract, he should be forced to abide by its provisions. But why should the employer have to honor a contract that was signed under duress? Suppose I held a gun on you, threatened to shoot you unless you signed a "contract" with me, promising to give me $100 per week. Later on, when you were safe, you reneged on this "contract." Certainly, you'd be within your rights.

7. Maximize Income

One reader asked: "How else is a man who sells the only product most of us have, labor and time, going to maximize the return of his investment, other than by joining a union?"

First of all, even if this were true, any criminal could say no less. A hold-up man, too, wants to "maximize the return of his investment" and does so by committing aggression against non-aggressors. How is the unionist any different than the hold-up man in this regard?

Second, it is by no means clear that organized labor is the last best chance for economic well being on the part of the workingman. Anyone ever hear of the rust belt? Unions from Illinois to Massachusetts demanded wages and fringe benefits in excess of productivity levels, and employers were powerless to resist. The result was "runaway shops." Either they ran into bankruptcy, or they relocated to places like Alabama, Mississippi, and Louisiana, where unionism was seen more for the economic and moral scourge that it is, than in Taxachussetts. If organizing workers into unions is the be all and end all of prosperity, how is it that wages and working conditions are very good in computers, insurance, banking, and a plethora of other non-unionized industries?

8. Hierarchy Is the Real Problem

This claim must have been made by a left-wing libertarian. He acknowledges that unions are illegitimate, but thinks that their real problem is that they are hierarchical, and chides me for not opposing *all* hierarchical organizations, which would certainly include employers, too.

But this is just plain silly. Libertarians oppose the initiation of coercion or the threat thereof, not hierarchy. Yes, all groups that violate the non-aggression axiom of libertarians are hierarchical. Governments, gangs, rapists, impose their will, by force, on their victims. They give orders. And yes, in all hierarchies, people at the top of the food chain give orders to those below them. But the difference, and this is crucial, is that the recipients of orders in the latter case have *agreed* to accept them, but this does not at all apply in the former case.

When the rapist orders the victim to carry out his commands, this is *illegitimate* hierarchy. When the conductor orders the cellist to do so, this is an aspect of *legitimate* hierarchy. I oppose unions not because they are hierarchical, but because the scabs have never agreed to carry out their orders.

CHAPTER 22

The Yellow Dog Contract; Bring Back This Heroic Institution[*]

The Yellow Dog Contract is an honorable contract. It states that one of the conditions of employment is that the worker agrees not to join a union. It is no different, in principle, from the requirement that if you come visit someone in his house at his invitation, you must wear a funny hat, or agree not to associate with anyone he specifies, say, an enemy of his. In each case, that of the firm, and the private home, the one making this "demand" is exercising his rights of free association. He is saying, in effect, "if you want to associate with me, you must do thus and such." You are perfectly free to refuse to do so, but then, he will not associate with you. He will not allow you into his home, nor agree to employ you.

But suppose you need a job? Is it not "unfair" that the employer will not hire you unless you give up, in advance, your rights to organize with others for better wages and working conditions? No; this situation is no more illicit than if you need to go to a party, and hate to wear a funny hat but the host insists upon it. Or demands, as the price of entry, that you not consort with his enemies. After all, it is *his* house.

We all assert our rights of free association through implicit "threats" of this sort. The wife says to the husband, "If you gamble away our money, I'll

[*]September 5, 2005.

leave you." The husband may say to the wife, "If you run around with other men, I'll divorce you." The customer says to the shopkeeper, "If you give me a bad product, you'll never see me in here again." The restaurant owner says to his diners, "If you can't behave yourself, I'll have to ask you to leave."

Free association is a crucially important element of liberty. Without the right to associate with those we (mutually) choose, we are in effect and to that extent, slaves. The *only* thing wrong with slavery was that the slave could not quit. He was forced to "associate" with the slave master against his will.

But the principle is the same with the Yellow Dog Contract. When it is banned, the employer is compelled to associate with a potential union member. To force him to do so is to coerce an innocent man. It is to violate his right to freely associate with others on a voluntary basis.

The argument for doing so is that without unions, wages would plummet to whatever low levels the "generosity" of employers would yield. But nothing could be further from the truth. Wages are, rather, determined on the basis of (marginal revenue) productivity, which in turn stems from how hard and smart we work, and with the cooperation of how much and of what quality capital equipment. Wages were rising long before the advent of unions in the early part of the twentieth century, in industries (computers, banking, insurance, baby sitting, lawn mowing) and countries (Hong Kong, Singapore, Taiwan) without any such labor organizations. Labor unions reached their apex decades ago, and now account for *single digits* in the private sector; during this sharp decrease in the proportion of workers "protected" by organized labor, wages catapulted.

No, labor organizations are instead an economic tapeworm, infesting firms and eating away their substance. It is no accident that what is now the "rust belt" in the northeastern quadrant of the country is the most heavily unionized sector of the nation, and suffered the greatest degree of plant closings when they were trying to suck the blood of entrepreneurs. Nor is it any puzzle that the south, the least unionized part of the country, became one of the fastest growing areas. Parasitical labor organizations in the coalfields were also responsible for the economic devastation of West Virginia.

Are unions per se illegitimate? No. If all they do is threaten mass quits unless their demands are met, they should not be banned by law. But as a matter of fact, not a one of them limits itself in this manner. Instead, in addition, they threaten the person and property not only of the owner, but also of any workers (they call them "scabs") who attempt to take up the wages and working conditions spurned by the union. They also favor labor legislation that compels the owner to deal with the union, when he wishes to ignore these workers and hire the "scabs" instead.

The Yellow Dog Contract, in addition to safeguarding employer and employee rights of free association, also serves as a remedy against union inflicted economic disarray and violence against innocent people and their property. Long live the Yellow Dog Contract. Bring it back. Now.

CHAPTER 23

Stop Whining About Jobs; It's Production That Counts*

A Primer on Jobs and the Jobless

With the economics of employment and unemployment constantly discussed on the business pages and in political campaigns, let us turn our attention toward fundamentals and root out some fallacies.

If the media tell us that "the opening of XYZ mill has created 1,000 new jobs," we give a cheer. When the ABC company closes and 500 jobs are lost, we're sad. The politician who can provide a subsidy to save ABC is almost assured of widespread public support for his work in preserving jobs.

But jobs in and of themselves do not guarantee well-being. Suppose that the employment is to dig huge holes and fill them up again. What if the workers manufacture goods and services that no one wants to purchase? In the Soviet Union, which boasted of giving every worker a job, many jobs were just this unproductive. Production is everything, and jobs are nothing but a means toward that end.

"We must not allow government to create jobs or we lose the goods and services that otherwise would have come into being."

---

*September 7, 2011 in *The Free Market*.

Imagine the Swiss Family Robinson marooned on a deserted South Sea island. Do they need jobs? No, they need food, clothing, shelter, and protection from wild animals. Every job created is a deduction from the limited, precious labor available. Work must be rationed, not created, so that the market can create the most products possible out of the limited supply of labor, capital goods, and natural resources.

The same is true for our society. The supply of labor is limited. We must not allow government to create jobs or we lose the goods and services that otherwise would have come into being. We must reserve precious labor for the important tasks still left undone.

Alternatively, imagine a world where radios, pizzas, jogging shoes, and everything else we might want continuously rained down like manna from heaven. Would we want jobs in such a utopia? No, we could devote ourselves to other tasks — studying, basking in the sun, etc., — that we would undertake for their intrinsic pleasure.

Instead of praising jobs for their own sake, we should ask why employment is so important. The answer is, because we exist amidst economic scarcity and must work to live and prosper. That's why we should be of good cheer *only* when we learn that this employment will produce things people actually value, i.e., are willing to buy with their own hard-earned money. And this is something that can only be done in the free market, not by bureaucrats and politicians.

But what about unemployment? What if people want to work but can't get a job? In almost every case, government programs are the cause of joblessness.

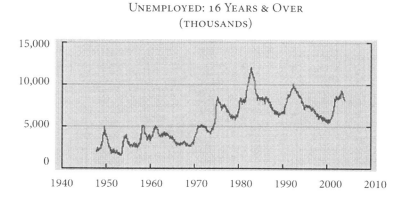

UNEMPLOYED: 16 YEARS & OVER
(THOUSANDS)

Minimum Wage

The minimum wage mandates that wages be set at a government-determined level. To explain why this is harmful, we can use an analogy from biology: there are certain animals that are weak compared to others. For example, the porcupine is defenseless except for its quills, the deer vulnerable except for its speed.

In economics there are also people who are relatively weak. The disabled, the young, minorities, the untrained — all are weak economic actors. But like the weak animals in biology, they have a compensating advantage: the ability to work for lower wages. When the government takes this ability away from them by forcing up pay scales, it is as if the porcupine were shorn of its quills. The result is unemployment, which creates desperate loneliness, isolation, and dependency.

Consider a young, uneducated, unskilled person, whose productivity is $2.50 an hour in the marketplace. What if the legislature passes a law requiring that he be paid $5 per hour? The employer hiring him would lose $2.50 an hour.

Consider a man and a woman each with a productivity of $10 per hour, and suppose, because of discrimination or whatever, that the man is paid $10 per hour and the woman is paid $8 per hour. It is as if the woman had a little sign on her forehead saying, "Hire me and earn an extra $2 an hour."

This makes her a desirable employee even for a sexist boss. But when an equal-pay law stipulates that she must be paid the same as the man, the employer can indulge his discriminatory tendencies and not hire her at all — at no cost to himself.

Comparable Worth

What if government gets the bright idea that nurses and truck drivers ought to be paid the same wage because their occupations are of "intrinsically" equal value? It orders that nurses' wages be raised to the same level, which creates unemployment for women.

Working Conditions

Laws that force employers to provide certain types of working conditions also create unemployment. For example, migrant fruit and vegetables pickers must have hot and cold running water and modern toilets in the temporary cabins provided for them. This is economically equivalent to wage laws because, from the point of view of the employer, working conditions are almost indistinguishable from money wages. And if the government forces him to pay more, he will have to hire fewer people.

UNIONS

When the government forces businesses to hire only union workers, it discriminates against non-union workers, causing them to be at a severe disadvantage or permanently unemployed. Unions exist primarily to keep out competition. They are a state-protected cartel like any other.

EMPLOYMENT PROTECTION

Employment-protection laws, which mandate that no one can be fired without due process, are supposed to protect employees. However, if the government tells the employer that he must keep the employee no matter what, he will tend not to hire him in the first place. This law, which appears to help workers, instead keeps them from employment. And so do employment taxes and payroll taxes, which increase costs to businesses and discourage them from hiring more workers.

PAYROLL TAXES

Payroll taxes like Social Security impose heavy monetary and administrative costs on businesses, drastically increasing the marginal cost of hiring new employees.

UNEMPLOYMENT INSURANCE

Government unemployment insurance and welfare cause unemployment by subsidizing idleness. When a certain behavior is subsidized — in this case not working — we get more of it.

LICENSING

Regulations and licensing also cause unemployment. Most people know that doctors and lawyers must have licenses. But few know that ferret breeders, falconers, and strawberry growers must also have them. In fact, government regulates over 1,000 occupations in all 50 states. A woman in Florida who ran a soup kitchen for the poor out of her home was recently shut down as an unlicensed restaurant, and many poor people now go hungry as a result.

When the government passes a law saying certain jobs cannot be undertaken without a license, it erects a legal barrier to entry. Why should it be illegal for anyone to try their hand at haircutting? The market will supply all the information consumers need.

When the government bestows legal status on a profession and passes a law against competitors, it creates unemployment. For example, who lobbies for the laws that prevent just anyone from giving a haircut? The haircutting industry — not to protect the consumer from bad haircuts but to protect themselves against competition.

PEDDLING

Laws against street peddlers prevent people from selling food and products to people who want them. In cities like New York and Washington, D.C., the most vociferous supporters of anti-peddling laws are established restaurants and department stores.

CHILD LABOR

There are many jobs that require little training — such as mowing lawns — that are perfect for young people who want to earn some money. In addition to the earnings, working also teaches young people what a job is, how to handle money, and how to save and maybe even invest. But in most places, the government discriminates against teenagers and prevents them from participating in the free-enterprise system. Kids can't even have a street-corner lemonade stand.

THE FEDERAL RESERVE

By bringing about the business cycle, Federal Reserve money creation causes unemployment. Inflation not only raises prices; it also misallocates labor. During the boom phase of the trade cycle, businesses hire new workers, many of whom are pulled from other lines of work by the higher wages. The Fed subsidy to these capital industries lasts only until the bust. Workers are then laid off and displaced.

THE FREE MARKET

The free market, of course, does not mean utopia. We live in a world of differing intelligence and skills, of changing market preferences, and of imperfect information, which can lead to temporary, market-generated unemployment, which Mises called "catallactic." And some people choose unemployment by holding out for a higher-paying job.

But as a society, we can ensure that everyone who wants to work has a chance to do so by repealing minimum-wage laws, comparable-worth rules, working-condition laws, compulsory union membership, employment protection, employment taxes, payroll taxes, government unemployment insurance, welfare, regulations, licensing, anti-peddling laws, child-labor laws, and government money creation. The path to jobs that matter is the free market.

III.

Personal Liberties

CHAPTER 24

Four Firemen Die in Socialist Fire; Worse, Two of Them Were Woman[*]

The headline in the newspaper was a horrendous one: Wildfire kills 4 firefighters in N. Cascades. Pictured was Pete Soderquist, the fire management officer in charge on the Cascade Mountains in central Washington state, who explained that the deaths were due to "when what had been a five-acre fire exploded into a wall of flame that trapped the crew." Also featured in photographs were the four firemen who perished: 30-year-old Tom Craven, 18-year-old Karen Fitzpatrick, 21-year-old Devin Weaver, and 19-year-old Jessica Johnson, all who lived in either Ellensburg or Yakima, Washington.

Any time there is a death of a human being, it is a tragedy (the reaction of the over-populationists to the contrary notwithstanding). When this occurs for any reason other than old age, this is even worse. When death is not instantaneous, and not painless, this is worse yet. When this occurs to four people in the prime of their lives — they were, respectively 30, 18, 21 and 19 years old — the degree of catastrophe rises even more, in view of the now never to be seen potential these four youngsters might have attained had they lived.

So far, these comments are pretty conventional. Very few would demur. But there are two controversial points to be made about this episode, both of which may teach important lessons.

---

[*]July 27, 2001.

First, this calamity occurred on public property, not private. The flames that consumed these four people took place in the Okanogan and Wenatchee National Forests, and are believed to have been set near Thirty Mile campground, another example of socialized land ownership. Now I am not saying that no deaths occur on private property. I do not maintain that these particular occurrences would necessarily have been avoided were these lands under private control.

However, the two are not unrelated, either. When a forest fire consumes private timber, there are individuals who feel it in their bank accounts; this is not the case with socialized land holdings. This means that the incentives are greater, by how much is an empirical matter, for profit making individuals to take greater precautions regarding their property than is true for their public counterparts. If we have learned anything from the fall of the Soviet economic system — and this is a highly debatable point — it is that things work better under private ownership. These four young people will have not died totally in vain if we use their deaths as a rallying cry for privatization of the forest. Perhaps if we succeed in this effort, other lives will be saved.

Second, there were two females amongst the death toll in this fire. I see their smiling faces shining out at me from the newspaper coverage of this event. Both young girls were very pretty.

There was a time in our past when no such thing could have occurred; when firefighting (along with other such dangerous activities as mining, policing, soldiering, lumberjacking, deep sea fishing, etc.) was the total province of men. Women and children died in calamities to be sure, but only if they were caught up in them as victims. Nowadays, with our modern dispensations, we place females in the front lines.

This is no less than an abomination. Females are far more precious than males. It is not for nothing that farmers keep a few bulls and hundreds of cows. It is due to patriarchy that we owe our very existence as a species. Imagine if our cavemen ancestors had sent their women out to hunt and face the lions and tigers when they came a-calling, instead of throwing themselves at these enemies, sacrificing themselves so that mankind could persist. After World War II, the adult male population of Germany, Russia, and other countries that suffered the most from the fighting was virtually wiped out. Yet the next generation, thanks to the relatively few men who survived, was able to come into being as if those losses had never occurred. Imagine if this war was fought primarily by the fairer sex; there would have been virtually no next generation. It cannot be denied that biologically speaking, men are in effect expendable drones.

So let us use the unfortunate deaths of these two young girls to resolve to turn back the clock to an earlier day when women were treated the way they should be treated. Let us return from "firefighters" to "firemen." Let us no longer blithely acquiesce in the senseless slaughter of precious females. Let us, instead, place them back up on that "pedestal" from which the so-called feminist movement has thrown them.

Now, of course, in a free society, people should be able to hire whomever they choose. Females should not be prohibited from trying to enter dangerous professions. And, of course, there are certain police jobs for which only women are by nature qualified to fill: e.g., prison guard in a female facility (but not to help wipe out prostitution, which should be legalized in any case). So this plea that we use the deaths of these two young Cascade women as an inspiration for ensuring the safety of future generations cannot be done through compulsion. But at the very least let us rescind all laws which require equal representation, or "balance." This should be done in all occupations, but let us at least begin with the dangerous ones. Freedom of association is not only just, it will promote the survival of our species as well.

CHAPTER 25

Arm the Coeds*

A
ccording to police and newspaper reports there has been a spate of robberies and sexual assaults aimed at university coeds in uptown New Orleans. A single black man approaches girls walking in the street in pairs at night and then proceeds to rob, confine, and sexually assault them.

The reaction on the part of the police authorities is the usual blather about being "street smart," not carrying a weapon, not resisting, and not venturing out at night. If going unarmed was such great advice, why don't they follow it themselves? Further, why should the *victims* have to pay twice, once in the form of being robbed and raped, and then, again, in the form of having their liberties to walk on the public streets curtailed?

The response from school authorities is, if anything, even worse: holding candlelight vigils, praying, having "take back the night" marches, and organizing teach-ins attempting to indoctrinate the students with the usual leftist feminist and liberal shibboleths, *ad nauseam*. If these things give university students any comfort, it is a *false* sense of security, which could prove to be their undoing. Quite possibly the assailant joins the very parade setup against him, biting his lip to keep from laughing outright, which might well be the only harm that befalls him from these events. Such tactics might make some people feel good, but they do nothing to address the problem.

---

*November 10, 2001.

In contrast, we offer a five-point program of arming the victims, virtually guaranteed to solve the problem.

1. Take down those signs on campuses announcing they are "gun-free" zones. That is the worst possible message to be sent to potential perpetrators of violence against our community. We might as well post a sign saying, "C'mon in, attackers, we've disarmed ourselves and will be easy prey." This no-gun policy, thank God, does not apply to campus police who can't be everywhere, as is the case with their city counterparts.

2. Require that all female students own a pistol or other means of self-defense; (e.g., pepper spray or mace, stun gun or other electric shock device) and carry it with them at all times. The women of Kennesaw, Georgia, an affluent northern suburb of Atlanta, Georgia, were once plagued by rapists. This town not only allowed, but *required* its citizens to be armed. You'll never guess what happened to the rape rate after this progressive policy was enacted.

The law, however, was compulsory, and, as such, violated the rights of pacifists and other local citizens who might have objected. But this would not at all apply to Loyola, a private institution. This change in policy would have to be "grand-fathered in" so as to avoid contractual violations, but in the future females who do not wish to protect themselves in this way would be perfectly free to attend other universities. They would have no right to be on campus, unless they obey all rules and regulations (in contrast, the citizenry of Kennesaw *did* have a right to remain there, in violation of the law). In the meantime, this enlightened policy could be introduced on a voluntary basis, and encouraged by the administration.

3. Packing a weapon is necessary, but not sufficient. All women at Loyola ought to be required to take a course in gun safety. The last thing we want are accidental shootings. Leftists bruit about statistics on accidents where children are killed with revolvers. But these data are wildly exaggerated by including the shooting deaths of young, teenaged gangbangers, whose deaths are certainly purposeful.

4. Volleyball, basketball, cross country, and baseball teams are all well and good, but a sports organization aimed at improving marksmanship would be far more helpful in present circumstances. (When is the last time a Loyola student won an Olympic medal in target shooting? Never, that's when. It is time, it is long past time, for a change.) All students don't have to be sharp shooters. Reasonable accuracy even at 10 to 15 feet will be more than enough to scare off potential rapists. Heck, even the presence of an automatic in a coed's handbag or pocket fully accomplishes this task.

5. When the new student center at Loyola is erected, it should include an indoor shooting range, just as the old field house did. The new rifle and pistol team would practice there, as would every woman student who so wished. The muffled sounds of target practice would alone give pause to all ne'er-do-wells in the neighborhood.

It will undoubtedly be objected against this "modest proposal" that arming young girls will not protect them; that their weapons will be seized by their attackers. Logic, common sense, and vast hordes of empirical evidence give the lie to all such negativism. Put yourself in the position of a New Orleans mugger and rapist: would you really want to engage in your usual depredations in the uptown area, knowing full well that you could do so on no more than even terms? Not bloody likely. The uptown predator has already come armed; let his victims face him on even terms. As to the facts of the matter, world-class economist John Lott has done a series of studies linking gun ownership with *increased* personal safety.

After this forward-looking policy proves a success in the collegiate uptown area, it could be implemented by private organizations throughout the entire city. Then and only then would the scourge of raping and robbing have a good chance of being vastly decreased throughout our whole community.

CHAPTER   26

Don't Take Your Daughter To Work and Other Un-PC Thoughts*

When Murray Rothbard was asked to account for his writing output, he would sometimes reply, "Hatred is my muse." By this he meant that he would read something — a book, an article, an op-ed, whatever — and he would be filled with a loathing for its content. He would be almost driven to blast away at it, swearing a mighty oath that the offending verbiage would not be allowed to stand unanswered.

Right now I have in front of me a piece by *Newsweek* sob sister Anna Quindlen extolling the virtues of Take Our Daughters to Work Day. While I don't mean to equate my output with Rothbard's writing, certainly not with the sheer enormity of it, to say nothing of its quality, something of the same reaction is welling up in me. If I read any more of this sort of thing, I think I'll be sick. It's either that or criticize it, however unaccustomed I am to such a role. Accordingly, I shall attempt to at least start the process of peeling away some of the many fallacies and pretensions of the feminists who argue in this way. Not that Miss (sic!) Quindlen is the worst offender of this ilk, but as the wrap-up writer for every second issue of *Newsweek*, she certainly reaches a large audience. Hence, a few critical remarks.

1. There is nothing wrong with taking children — both girls and boys — to work to see what their parents are up to on Monday through Friday,

---

*June 6, 2002. Co-authored with William Barnett II.

9–5. If the kids can more easily picture their parents while separated from them, this cannot help but be all to the good. But surely this applies *equally* to boys and girls.

Even here, however, there are problems. For one thing, why is it that there are so many mothers who have abandoned their children, many at very tender ages? If poverty has engendered this decision, well and good. But all too often this stems either from feminist ideology ("work good, motherhood bad;" "we can too have it all"), or from the avaricious nature of the modern state, which has raised taxes to such unconscionable levels that both parents are often forced to work.

2. Another motive for taking the kiddies to work is to get them acclimated to this activity. Here, the case is far less compelling. For one thing, it is way too premature, especially for the very young. For another, there is always the danger that the lesson learned will be that the kids should follow in their parent's footsteps, not with regard to work in general, but rather that specific type of employment. This is problematic because the well-being of the next generation depends upon their making their own way in this regard. There is nothing more sad than picking a career not based upon personal likes and dislikes, but rather on the basis of following in the footsteps of someone else. Of course, one Take Your Kids to Work Day per year is unlikely to lead to any such result, except for fanatics, such as populate the women's "liberation" movement.

3. But assume, for the sake of argument, that introducing children to the world of work has unambiguous good effects. Who should have preference in this regard, given that for some reason this must be done, males or females? Members of the feminist cult will froth at the mouth that such a question should even be raised (that's no news; they have this emotional reaction to *anything or anyone* disagreeing with their party line) but they themselves started this by organizing a day at the office or factory for only one gender.

To ask this question is to answer it: boys should have preference over girls. After all, it is man, not woman, who will spend the lion's share of their adult life behind a desk, or on an assembly line. It is women, not men, who will take time out to raise the next generation, if there is to be one, a less than certain state of affairs if feminists get their way.

How many women's lives have been immiserated, when they follow the siren song of equality between the sexes, of the "we can have it all" school, only to arrive, childless, at early middle age, when certain options are forever foreclosed? Ask not for whom the clock ticks; it ticks for thee!

To avoid this horrendous fate, both individually and for the species as a whole (although it cannot be counted as totally bad that the genes of these foolish women will be less likely to be passed on), little girls ought to be taught homemaking, cooking and make-up application, the better to attract a husband. Now, no one is calling for "barefoot, pregnant and in the kitchen," and for less than full attachment to the labor force, on a coercive basis, through law. But as generations of experience have shown, this is not an altogether bad recipe for personal happiness on the part of women and species survival (the lefties seem more worried about the extinction of any and all species with the exception of our own).

4. But what about the "glass ceiling," feminists, including Miss Quindlen ("the Senate is still 87 percent male," she wails) are always decrying? Won't Take Our Daughters to Work Day (and dozens of other such programs) at least put a dent in this injustice?

Not at all. Females are under-represented in the highest reaches of law, politics, Nobel prizes, chess grand master rankings, IQ, SAT and ACT scores, etc., not because of male plotting, nor discrimination, nor yet general injustice. Rather, this stems, mainly, from biological considerations. Yes, the normal or bell curve for male and female ability (as measured, say, by IQ) peaks at around the same point. This is why, barring the asymmetric effects of marriage, male and female incomes are indistinguishable, on average. (Marriage raises male incomes and reduces those of females, due to the unequal sharing of household tasks, labor force participation rates, time spent on child rearing, etc. The evidence? There is no pay gap whatsoever for never-marrieds; zero; nada.) But the variances between men and women are very different. Relatively more females cluster around the mean (*YX*). Proportionately, males are all over the lot (*XY*). If women are God's (or evolution's) insurance policy, then men are the crap shoot. It is for this reason that men but not women, in the main, have been able to rise above the "glass ceiling" (*A*), and that women but not men are rarely found below "hell's floor" (*D*), to coin a phrase. Go to any prison, mental institution, or homeless shelter, and count the numbers of men (*C*) and women (*D*) on the left tail of the bell curve. The former outnumber the latter by roughly the same proportions that hold true on the right side of the normal curve in the boardroom, or in the executive suite, or in the president's office, or on the battle field (*A* vs. *B*). (The curves are drawn freehand so as to exaggerate the differences between male and female standard deviations for purposes of illustration.)

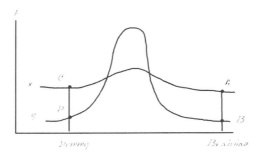

Moreover, there are good and sufficient sociobiological reasons why this should be so, which stem from requirements for the survival of the human species (something very far removed from the concerns of the feminists): it takes far fewer males than females to create the next generation. It is not for nothing that the farmer keeps 50 cows and 1 bull, not the reverse. Biologically speaking, if there were 50 bulls to go along with a like number of cows 49 of the former would be superfluous, and the reverse does not hold at all.

If human males are heterodox in their abilities, and there is a bias in favor of the genes of the smarter ones (strictly speaking, those whose survival until child rearing age is more likely for whatever reason) then great male but not female variation improves the quality of the human herd. This argument does not apply to females, since they are the bottleneck when it comes to raising the next generation. That is, with the usual proportion of 50 cows and one bull, not a single one of the former is superfluous, so there are no particular gains if they vary greatly in ability.

Imagine two tribes of ancient humans, otherwise identical, except that one was like our own, and the other had a great variation in female, but not male abilities. Which would out compete the other insofar as improvements in the gene pool were concerned? Ours would, since virtually all the females who wished to could become impregnated (this was before the era of feminism), while mainly the superior males would supply the sperm. In the other tribe, again virtually all of the females would become pregnant, if the tribe is to survive, but very few of the fathers would be "superior" types, since by stipulation, there are few such in this tribe. Thus, our tribe is eugenic, and survived, while, relatively speaking, this other tribe was dysgenic, and becomes extinct.

CHAPTER 27

Feminist Sports Fraud; High School Boys Are Better Than the Top Women Athletes[*]

Annika Sorenstam has accepted her invitation to play in the men's Professional Golf Association tournament in Fort Worth, Texas, and everyone and his uncle (excuse me, his aunt) has practically dropped their teeth over this wondrous occurrence.

Headlines range from "Let's hear it for Sorenstam," to "She's an inspiration," to "Why this Swede is 'da woman' of golf." If there has been a critical reaction to this phenomenon in the mainstream press, I have not heard about it.

Her first day 71 score (one over par) at the Bank of America Colonial was good enough to beat out or tie several of her male competitors. This set off even more paroxysms of self-congratulation and high-fiving amongst the politically correct sports commentators. According to one low-key journalist, this accomplishment "made golf fans around the world scream with joy." Another has even gone so far as to characterize Annika's accomplishment "as one of the all-time greatest performances by a female athlete in any sport." There may be a glass ceiling in the business world (that is a bit of economic illiteracy that shall have to be discussed on another occasion), but the "grass ceiling" in athletics in general, and golf in particular, seems to have been pierced.

---

[*]May 24, 2003; statistics compiled by Dan D'Amico and Erich Mattei.

Before we get caught up in the general hysteria, let us recognize a few worms in this particular apple. If females can enter male competitions on the grounds that they are just as good as men, then, based on this egalitarian "logic," the latter will no longer be able to be kept out of those that have previously been limited to women. After all, why have different sections of an athletic event, if there are no relevant differences? No one organizes special matches for left- and right-handed people, for the blue eyed and the brown eyed, because these differences are not thought to be relevant to ability. If the internal plumbing of human beings is now likewise determined to be of no moment, competitively speaking, thanks to Annika's marvelous accomplishments, why, then, there would be no reason to preclude males from female competitions. There would no longer be separate track and field, swimming, basketball, golfing, or tennis leagues for men and women. In this one size fits all new world order, all separations between the LPGA and the PGA, between the NBA and the WNBA would disappear. Segregation, after all, is invidious.

But this would pretty much spell the death knell for women's sports. With the possible exception of sports that call more for finesse than strength (think billiards, bowling, and, ok, maybe, golf), females would be all but frozen out of professional top-flight competition (and even here, it would be the rare woman who could effectively compete with men). In the present left-wing feminist frenzy, this may not be readily apparent in basketball, tennis, soccer, baseball, and other team sports. The two genders rarely if ever meet each other in sanctioned official matches. Although even here, there is some supportive evidence. E.g., the top speed for a male tennis serve is 149 mph; the female counterpart is only 127.4 mph. Yes, yes, (a young) Billie Jean King beat (an old) Bobby Riggs in a tennis match. This is just the exception that proves the rule.

However, there is a plethora of data, emanating from sports in which success can be measured objectively, which indicates that few or no women would be able to compete effectively against men. For example:

- The high jump world record for men is 8'5"; for women it is only 6/10'.25. In contrast, the boys' high school record is 7'6."

- The best male long jump is 29'4.5"; the top female can do only 24'8." The long jump record in high school (male, of course) is 26'9.25."

- The mile can be run by a male athlete in 3:43.1; a female takes 4:12.6; a high schooler can do this distance in 3:53.

- The male record for the 100-meter run is 9.78 seconds, the female, 10.49; the high school record is 10.13.

Forget competing against world-class male athletes; the top women would not even be able to garner medals in a robust high school setting.

This pattern of male dominance holds true for all sports where a premium is enjoyed by possessing strength, speed, and endurance. And in quite a few "sports" where it is not. For example, this applies to virtually all chess grandmasters.

These points are made not to demonstrate male superiority in athletics. Their dominance is so well established by the facts, that only hysterical left-wing feminists (of both sexes) must be reminded of them. No. We take cognizance of them because of the danger to *women's sports*, posed by allowing Annika Sorenstam to compete with men. If we are logically consistent, and allow the genders to play against each other in such environments, there will *be* (virtually) no athletic contests where girls and women will have any chance of victory.

In boxing and other martial arts, there are commonly weight divisions. This doesn't mean that a pugilist weighing 120 pounds can never triumph over someone at the 190-pound level. We engage in such segregation because weight gives such a clear advantage to the heavier athlete, other things equal, that a match between two such competitors would be too one-sided. It would be boring to watch. Most people would consider it "unfair."

It is precisely the same with men and women.

CHAPTER 28

Term Limits Hurt Female Politicians; A Silver Lining*

L et us consider the silver lining involved in term limits: it reduces (this is *not* a misprint) the percentage of female politicians.

There is much wailing and gnashing of teeth at this phenom-enon on the part of our friends on the Democratic side of the aisle. According to an editorial appearing in the *Seattle Times* (okay, okay, this statement doesn't appear on the editorial pages, but rather is disguised as "news"): "Fewer female legislators in statehouses: Term limits are seen as culprit in curtailing women's progress in winning seats, which has stalled since the early 1990s." The editorial, sorry, the story, goes on to say that in states with term limits, female politicians are very rare. For example, 9.4 percent of South Carolina legislators were female, in Alabama it was 10 percent, and in Kentucky the figure was 10.9 percent. In contrast, in the non-term limit states, the percentages were much higher. E.g., 36.7 percent in Washington, 52 percent in Michigan, 33 percent in both Colorado and Maryland. (The overall average in 2003 was 22.3 percent, down from a high of 22.7 percent in 2002.)

So much for the facts. Where is the silver lining?

In order for there to be a silver lining, there has to be an evil, and, also, some good must come out of it. I am already on record (see chapter 45) in taking the position that term limits are highly problematic. I did so on ground blazed by Professor Hans Hoppe. His argument is based on time

---

*September 3, 2003.

preference: other things equal, the longer a politician is in office, the more of a long-run viewpoint he can afford to take. If he can leave the office to his children (e.g., a monarchy) he will act even more responsibly; he doesn't want to kill the golden goose, otherwise there will be nothing left for his progeny to exploit.

In the other direction, if a politician could only be in office for, say, one month, then "make hay while the sun shines," even more so than at present, would become his motto. That is, he would have very little incentive to rein in his natural rapaciousness, for he would be turned out all too soon. There would only be the thinnest veneer of "public service" to cover the theft-as-usual policies. Why leave much of anything for the next officeholder, certainly not if it interferes with your own pillage?

Term limits, then, are a disaster, in that they enhance the already very great incentives for politicians to loot.

But there is a silver lining: females appear to be booted out by this initiative to an even greater degree than males. Why is this to be considered a good thing?

On the economic front, it is clear that women on average favor social welfare schemes more than men, and I extrapolate from females in general to their sister politicians. It is surely no accident that programs such as social security, welfare, and unemployment insurance came after the "weaker sex" was given the right to vote. This phenomenon might stem from women being more risk averse than men, and seeing such coercive socialistic policies as somehow "safer."

Further evidence: there is a large "gender gap" between the Republican and Democratic parties on domestic issues; females favor the latter over the former; as well, the membership of the Libertarian Party is overwhelmingly male. (As against this, I must concede that on matters of imperialism and foreign military adventurism, female timidity probably inclines them to a less aggressive stance.)

Second, apart from considerations of this sort, there is no intrinsic reason to favor male over female politicians. With the exception of Ron Paul and only a few others, all are hypocritical and pompous mountebanks, not content with merely robbing us, but determined to convince us they do it for our own good. However, another issue arises: one of the strongest motivating forces behind the leftish push for female politicians is the quaint notion that apart from underhanded skullduggery, all groups would be exactly equal. That is, in the truly just society, both genders, all races and nationalities, all ages, people of all sexual orientations, etc., bloody, etc., would be equally represented in all callings. If they are not, this is due to exploitation, or injustice, or some such. That is, absent improprieties such as racism, sexism, look-ism (I kid you not), able-ism, etc., since males and females comprise roughly 50 percent each of the electorate, this would also be their representation amongst office holders. (Also, the National Basketball Association would employ as players tall strong athletic blacks, and short fat Jews, in proportion to their overall numbers in the population; it is only due to racial discrimination against Orientals that so few of them are on National Football League team rosters.)

There is no one who has done more to combat this pernicious fallacy than Tom Sowell. (See this, among his many excellent books, *Race and Culture.*) But he needs all the help he can get on this mission. It is incumbent upon all men of good will to help him in this regard. And one way that we can do so is to recognize one of the side order benefits of that otherwise insidious policy of term limits: that it disproportionately penalizes female politicians.

To clarify matters. I do *not* favor term limits. However, I do recognize that there is a silver lining in this particular cloud.

B. Drugs

CHAPTER 29

Second Thoughts on Drug Legalization: It Means More Loot For the State*

Don't get me wrong. I am entirely and totally committed to the legalization of drugs. This includes *all* addictive substances, not just marijuana. When they write about drugs, most libertarians favor legalization. I am enough of an iconoclast to consider the case in behalf of prohibition (on libertarian grounds, of course). But, don't worry, I come out on this issue on the correct side.

There are many good and sufficient reasons for this stance, none of which concern us today, since I wish, now, to discuss, not justifications for legalization, but, rather, one argument for prohibition, and one *against* legalization.

What then is the argument against legalization? Paradoxically, it is one often made by non-libertarians in *favor* of decriminalization. The argument goes as follows: right now, addictive drugs can only be bought and sold on the black market. As such, the government obtains no tax revenues thereby, since all these transactions are entirely off the books. However, if this industry were but recognized as a legitimate one, then its products could be taxed, just as in the case of all legal goods and services. Thus, the government could obtain more revenues than at present. And this in turn would mean either a reduction in other taxes, a lower deficit, more government services, or some combination of all three.

---

*August 12, 2003.

Any argument the conclusion of which is that the government will have more revenues at its disposal is highly problematic. For the libertarian, this is pretty much a refutation. For the state already has too much of our money, far too much. The last thing it needs is more encouragement, in the form of greater income. Yes, drugs should still be legalized, since their use and sale does not violate the libertarian non-aggression axiom, but this should occur *in spite* of the fact that the tax take will rise, not *because* of it.

If, as a result, there is a reduction in other taxes, it is not readily apparent why this should be an unambiguous gain for liberty. All that would occur is that some people would pay more, and others less. If there is a lower deficit, this will even the more encourage the government in its profligate expenditure policies. Nor is an increase in government "services" an unequivocal gain, not for utility, let alone liberty. For virtually all state spending, even apart from the compulsory way in which it is financed, does far more harm than create benefit. One need only mention in this regard public schools which are educational cesspools, and foreign military adventurism which kill innocents in their thousands.

Let us now consider the second argument, that in favor of prohibition: it puts numerous criminals in jail who otherwise would not have been caught. According to some estimates, in the neighborhood of 40–60 percent of all inmates owe their present address to the drug laws. Some of them, probably, are guilty of no real libertarian crime at all: peacefully buying, selling, and using controlled substances. And with regard to such people, the drug laws are an unmitigated disaster, morally, legally, and economically. However, many of those incarcerated for drug violations are guilty of committing violent crimes, and a significant proportion of these would not be in jail but for the present prohibition of addictive substances.

Face it; the public police are an inept lot (see Murray Rothbard, *For a New Liberty*; and also Patrick Tinsley, "A Case for Private Police"). What else do you expect from an institution run on the same principles as public education, the army, the motor vehicle bureau, and the post office? Were there private police, they would undoubtedly be far more efficient. But there are not. Scared citizens, then, can be excused for appreciating the fact that the drug laws put numerous miscreants behind bars who would otherwise be free to roam the streets, pillaging, rioting, robbing, and raping, as is their wont.

To the extent, then, not that innocent people are imprisoned due to the drug laws, but that this applies, rather, to murderers, rapists and thieves who would not otherwise have been caught, it cannot be said that this legislation is all bad.

Gary Becker, for one, is not likely to much appreciate this argument. He maintains, to the contrary, that one of the horrors of prohibition is that so many denizens of the black inner cities are placed in jail, which wreaks havoc, he thinks, on this community. But if it is correct that a significant proportion of such people are really dangerous malefactors (even though found guilty in government courts for what libertarians would consider non-crimes), then this community, to say nothing of the rest of us, is far safer under present conditions.

Becker correctly sees the high rate of incarceration of blacks as causally connected to elevated rates of illegitimacy. But he states: "Unfortunately, some states still make it difficult for two-parent families to collect welfare." Evidently, this Nobel prize-winning economist thinks that welfare is a solution to, not a source of, the travails of the black community. He seems not to have read, or perhaps not fully appreciated, Charles Murray's *Losing Ground*, which shows that welfare is the *cause* of family breakdown, not the *solution* to this problem.

This is rather disappointing to those who look to the University of Chicago for free market solutions. Perhaps it is a case of mistaken identity to expect libertarian analysis to emanate from the Windy City's most famous university.

Let us conclude. I am not arguing in favor of drug prohibition. I favor legalization. But we should be aware that there are real drawbacks to this stance: more money for the government, and more (real) criminals running loose.

CHAPTER 30

The Libertarian Case For Drug Prohibition[*]

O k, ok, already, hold onto your horses. I have not given up on libertarianism. Nor have I finally, and completely, succumbed to Alzheimer's disease. It is just that since all of us who favor economic freedom oppose drug prohibition, the contentious part of my personality naturally looks around for reasons on the other side of this debate.

That, plus the fact that I had the unfortunate experience at a recent conference I attended of hearing a supposed libertarian "defend" drug legalization; he did so in such a manner that I didn't have to be particularly quarrelsome or defensive about libertarianism to oppose him. Moreover, the fact that this seminar was constructed in such a manner that I was not able to publicly criticize the outrageous case he offered made it all the more important that I somehow get this off my chest. You, gentle reader, will have to stand in for the audience I might have otherwise addressed.

So, what are the reasons, in general, for maintaining the status quo regarding the prohibition of addictive substances?

1. Without this law, our movies, television programming, plays, novels, and other vehicles of storytelling would be much less enriched than now they are. Award winning television series such as *Law and Order* and *The Sopranos* would be particularly hard hit by repeal. It is an exaggeration to say that programming of this ilk contains *nothing but* this motif, but not by much. Surely, at least half of the themes explored in the cops and robbers

---

[*]July 12, 2002.

genre depend upon the fact that there is a black market in marijuana, cocaine, and heroin.

2. Were addictive materials to be legalized a whole host of jobs would be lost. (Look, I said I would give *reasons* in support of prohibition; I did not say I would give *good* ones in this regard. As far as I am concerned, there *are* no good reasons. I am willing to defend the "undefendable," but this is not undefendable.) We are talking, here, about judges, policemen, jail guards, social workers, lawyers, district attorneys, psychologists, munitions makers, small planes, and boats, etc., bloody etc. Could it be that one of the strongest reasons for the retention of this horrid law is this self-same fact? I wonder. Not, of course, that jobs are needed. That is the unfortunate legacy of Keynes and Keynesianism. As every Austrian from Mises to Hazlitt to Rothbard has shown, it is not rational to create jobs merely for the sake of creating jobs. We could all be employed digging ditches and filling them in again, and would starve as a result. No, the whole point of jobs is to create goods and services of *value*, and the ones that come about as a result of drug prohibition hardly qualify.

What, then, are the obnoxious reasons offered by this "libertarian" in behalf of drug legalization?

3. The present drug laws bring about a general disrespect for law and order, and this is something to be greatly regretted. But this is highly problematic from the libertarian perspective. Thousands? Tens of thousands? Hundreds of thousands? But how many laws are there today? This is hard to determine. Probably no one knows to an exactitude, even as of any given date (there are new ones coming on board every day). It depends upon whether or not administrative decisions should be counted; and why not? If so, laws presumably number in the millions. Literally.

And, of these, how many are *good* laws, e.g., enactments compatible with the libertarian axiom of non-aggression? Well, let's see. There are laws against murder, theft, trespass, fraud, kidnapping, assault and battery, rape, … I am quickly running out of examples. Well, I suppose we can pick up a few more, possibly, from the Ten Commandments; and defense of contracts from the civil law. But that is about it.

So, it is pro-libertarian to promote a general respect for law? Hardly. Virtually all law is bad law. Only an infinitesimal percentage of all law is good law. Respecting law in general, then, is to promote evil. How, then, are we to regard favoring the repeal of drug laws on the grounds that they reduce respect for law in general? Whatever else may be said about this contention, it cannot be claimed that it is compatible with libertarianism.

4. The economist goes on and on, *ad nauseum*, about how he as an economist needs data for public policy analysis. Without data, he never tires of telling us, it is impossible to make an informed decision as to whether or not addictive substances should be legalized.

But this is stuff and nonsense. Whether or not drugs should be prohibited by law is a matter of *normative* economics. Data, in stark contrast, is part and parcel of *positive* economics. To be sure, in some moral systems, e.g., utilitarianism, the latter is not irrelevant to the former. But for the deontological libertarian, it comes down to a matter of *rights*. Does the (adult) individual have the right to inject into his body whatever he pleases, harmful or not? And the answer is, of course he does.

It is more than passing curious that this economics professor, after recounting the necessity of data, and bewailing its absence, nevertheless takes the pro-legalization side of this debate. Perhaps the statistics are not that necessary after all.

5. According to the speaker at this conference I am criticizing, the market price of a pound of marijuana is presently about $3,000. He estimates that the total costs under legalization would be something of the order of $3 per pound. Thus, the profit (plus the black market costs, given that this market is illegal) amount to some $2,997, or 99.9. percent of the total.

This speaker "doesn't like" the people who are presently enjoying this differential. He favors legalization, so that they will no longer have access to these funds. He full well realizes that when and if the government legalizes this product, it will tax the stuffing out of it, just as it presently does in the cases of booze and tobacco. He offers as yet another reason for legalizing marijuana that this will, in one fell swoop, take the profits away from the present producers.

Now I full well sympathize with this professor's assessment of your typical denizen of the drug market. He is mean and vicious, fully willing and able to use violence against police, competitors, sometimes even customers. It is thanks to him and his confreres that we have a new word to describe innocent victims of drug gang warfare: "mushrooms." His product is oft-time poisonous, and the dosage uncertain. These are altogether a pretty despicable lot of people. Of course, as is well known in the libertarian community, these characteristics stem, entirely, from the illegal status of drugs. During alcohol prohibition, the proprietors were similar to today's drug dealers. Nowadays, under legalization of beer, wine, and liquor, the purveyors are indistinguishable from those who manufacture cheese or chalk.

However, with whom are we comparing these very bad people? (Typical economist's joke; question: "How's your wife?" answer: "Compared to whom?") Answer: we are comparing them with the *government*! How many innocent people have all the drug gangs in the world murdered? A couple of hundred? A couple of thousand? A few tens of thousands? In contrast, according to R.J. Rummel, *Death By Government*, governments are responsible for killing no fewer than about 170 million of their own residents and citizens in the twentieth century; we are talking non-combatants here. This economist wants data? Here is data. What can we say about the moral status of a commentator who favors a public policy (partially) on the grounds that a gang responsible for a relative handful of deaths will be deprived of financial resources, and that they will be given over to a different gang of people who have killed millions?

Yes, by all means, let us legalize drugs. (I told you I'm still a libertarian.) And, perhaps, our plays and movies will be less dramatic. But there will be no gain from decriminalization concerning jobs, or respect for law, or better allocation of funds from drug gang to government gang.

C. Charity

CHAPTER 31

Celebrities Engaged in Legalized Theft[*]

M uhammad Ali had a storied career as a boxer, activist in the "black is beautiful" movement and anti-Viet Nam War protester. He inspired millions of people with his exploits inside and outside of the boxing ring.

Michael J. Fox brought great pleasure to millions of television viewers with his work on *Family Ties*, and then *Spin City*. He has also appeared in numerous movies, — who can ever forget the *Back to the Future* series? — to great critical and commercial acclaim. Then there is Christopher Reeves who has attained world renown for bringing Superman alive to us. His steely blue eyes, his red and blue uniform with the "S" on the chest, his cape, his deeds of derring-do, are a vital part of our culture.

In their past careers, these three men were stars. The entire nation, nay, virtually all of the civilized world, venerated them. Young people tried to emulate them in their own lives. Women would swoon whenever any of these three appeared.

Where are they now? Each, unfortunately, has been struck with a dread debilitation. Ali and Fox have contracted Parkinson's disease, and Reeves has been victimized by a spinal cord injury. But there have been moral lapses as well. Ali, Fox, and Reeves, along with many other professional

---

[*]May 24, 2002.

athletes and stars of stage and screen, have been actively engaged in inciting theft. To wit: they have testified before Congress, asking that money be allotted to the study and cure of these diseases and debilitations. If you don't believe this characterization, ask yourself: where will these monies come from?

Are Ali, Fox, and Reeves asking for voluntary contributions from willing charitable donors? Not a bit of it. Very much to the contrary, these funds will be demanded from taxpayers at the point of a gun. Yes, the purposes to which they will be put will be good ones. Who, after all, can oppose medical research, and support for the afflicted? But the road to hell is paved with good intentions; the devil is in the details. It does not suffice that the aims are good ones; the means must also be proper as well, and here they are not.

It cannot be denied that these celebrities have had great success in their booty seeking. They have already succeeded in raising vast sums of money not their own from politicians. And the indications are that there is more to come in future: yesterday, Michael J. Fox's testimony before a Senate committee was greeted by applause, an all but unprecedented occurrence in those "hallowed" halls.

This attempt to garner money against the will of their owners stands in very sharp contrast indeed with their earlier careers that brought them fame in the first place. There, not a penny was mulcted from unwilling donors. Every penny earned by Ali in the boxing ring came from fans who voluntarily plunked their money down on the barrel head to see him fight. The boxers pummeled by him in the ring agreed to be there, and were paid for their own efforts. In the cases of Fox and Reeves, here was not a single solitary movie-goer or television watcher who was forced to pay for these benefits; all participated in commercial endeavors with these actors on a completely voluntary basis.

So I beseech these actors, athletes, and other heroes of the culture: do not allow your names to be used in this nefarious manner. Return to your voluntary roots. Go back to the behavior which first made you famous: capitalist acts between consenting adults. Certainly, raise money to fight these debilitations! But do so in a civilized manner, not one befitting a thug. If you cease and desist from these evil acts, I personally promise to contribute to your charitable goals. Yes, there may at the end of the day be less money forthcoming for these noble purposes, but every penny of it will be legitimate.

CHAPTER **32**

Don't Donate
To the Red Cross*

I n chapter 16 and 17 I have written about hurricanes afflicting New Orleans, and my attempts as a resident of the Big Easy to escape from them; once on Ivan, and then on Katrina. The latter led to a good many responses.

There was plenty of positive response, but I will not reply to any of that, except to thank the readers for their warm support.

The negative reaction expressed two concerns; first that I was talking through my hat (the word "moron," and worse, kept cropping up) in terms of free enterprise being able to control the weather, and second that I was totally off-base in urging that people not contribute to the Red Cross, but instead to the Salvation Army for short-term needs (I thanked the sainted Wal-Mart Corporation for doing so), and to support the Mises Institute and the Libertarian Parties of Louisiana, Mississippi, and Alabama for long-term considerations.

Let me now reply to each of these issues.

I. CLOUD SEEDING

First, the weather (I owe a great debt of gratitude to Yang Chenping for steering me to the material I cite below in this section).

I concede to my critics that the free enterprise system is nowhere near to being able to quell category 5 hurricanes such as Katrina (she slowed

---

*September 12, 2005.

down to a category 4 level only when she reached the coast). However, there is at least such a thing as a weather control industry. It is viable. It is operational. It has made great strides already, and is continually improving. It is benefiting from the weeding out process, whereby firms that satisfy customers enlarge their scale of operation, and those that do not pass by the wayside. This is the recipe for success in every other industry known to man, and there is no reason to posit that it cannot, indeed, is not, functioning in this way at present in terms of weather control.

Consider in this regard Dyn-O-Mat, Inc. The stock in trade of this company, located in Riviera Beach, Florida, is to "implode" storms by seeding them with chemicals, and/or to at least reduce their severity. According to CEO Peter Cordani "attacking a pie-shaped sliver of a hurricane as it forms over water could slow the storm down by 15 to 20 mph, causing the winds to turn on themselves." He continued: "We're not going to get rid of the storm," he said. "There will still be heavy rain. We're just trying to take the punch out of it."

Then there is Weather Modification, Inc. This firm has been operating out of Fargo, North Dakota since 1961 and offers services in terms of "rainfall increase (rain enhancement), snow pack augmentation, hail damage mitigation (hail suppression), and fog clearing (fog dissipation)."

North American Weather Consultants, Inc., "incorporated in 1950, specializes in providing Weather Modification, Air Quality Services, Ambient Monitoring, Tracer Studies, (and) Applied Meteorological Studies."

"Research from the Great Barrier Reef off the Australian coast shows that corals are packed full of the chemical dimethyl sulphide, or DMS. When released into the atmosphere, DMS helps clouds to form, which could have a large impact on the local climate."

The Nissan Corporation protected its parking lot, chock full of automobiles, from a hailstorm by shooting off a cannon that sends "sonic waves up to 50,000 feet in the air." According to Eric Rademacher, an environmental engineer with Nissan, "Hailstones are formed and begin with a piece of dust in the clouds. There is a lot of activity going on, and what we do is to de-ionize that activity in the clouds and keep those dust particles from collecting moisture out of the clouds in turn reacting and forming what we know as a hailstone." Hailstones today, hopefully hurricanes tomorrow.

But all is not well regarding the private enterprise of weather control. Government is sticking its evil nose into the initiative. From 1962 until 1983, the National Weather Service was involved in such initiatives with its

Project Stormfury. But they gave up, and now bash private companies such as the ones above, who are attempting to improve matters.

Even that great bastion of free enterprise, China, has gotten into the act. According to a *China Daily* report "Drought-stricken central Henan province has been using a method called cloud seeding, in which chemicals are shot at clouds." The only problem here is that those responsible for these acts were not actually market participants; rather, they were elements of the government.

A similar threat to a complete role for private enterprise in protection against the elements emanates from Russia. In order to protect its sixtieth anniversary of its victory over Nazi Germany the Russian air force was dispatched to disperse rain clouds.

As well, the governments of Philippines, India, Thailand, New South Wales, and others, plus several U.S. states such as Utah, North Dakota, Nevada, Arizona, Kansas, Texas, and Colorado have gotten into the act. They, too, are horning in on what should ideally be entirely a private initiative. Perhaps the worst aspect of this is that the U.S. government is now contemplating getting back into this business. Weather socialism we can do without. (Happily, some such as Oklahoma seem to have suspended their involvement.) There is even a silver lining in the cloud of Moscow's celebration. Private individuals too, such as Paul McCartney, have entered the fray, kicking in "$55,000 for three jets to spray the clouds above the city with dry ice. Some 50,000 people gathered in Palace Square for McCartney's concert, only his second performance in Russia. The former Soviet regime had banned Beatle's music as a corrupting influence."

Personal disclosure. I have no stock in any cloud seeding or any other such company. I am an economist, not a meteorologist. I make no claim that this technology shall be the one that finally brings winds on steroids like Katrina to her knees. There are dangers in this technology, too. All I am saying is that the market — with proper protections for private property owners — can be trusted to satisfy consumers in this field as in all others.

Is there any doubt that if the government can keep its mitts off this industry, in the years to come it will make great strides in protecting us from inclement weather? But that means no excessive taxation, no unnecessary and stultifying regulation, no nationalization, and no subsidization of government bureaus in competition with these folks (such as the case in which public libraries compete with private bookstores and lending libraries, and even with your local neighborhood Block Buster.)

The technology of cloud seeding has been utilized since 1946. Vincent Schaefer of General Electric Labs was the pioneer in this regard. Private enterprise is not anywhere near perfecting it. But it is my contention that if government stays away, objections to the contrary notwithstanding, that this is the last best long-run hope for humanity to rid itself of this ancient scourge.

II. Charity

Let us now consider the issue of charity, in the aftermath of Katrina's devastation.

First, the short-run. Why do I continue to favor the Salvation Army? Mainly because the proportion of their donations spent on salaries, fund-raising, and administrative costs is very low. The overwhelming majority of the money entrusted to them is allocated to the purpose for which it is donated. Second, they cooperate with the sainted Wal-Mart Corporation, and no one who does that can be all bad.

How about the Red Cross? I have several things against them. Minor point: they are over bureaucratized. They turned down offers from numerous people anxious to offer help to the victims of Katrina. Then, as I mentioned before, they are so politically correct they did not sufficiently scrutinize the blood donations made by homosexuals, due to considerations of political correctness. As a result, innocent people contracted AIDS. Then, too, they are in far too close association with government for my tastes.

What about the long run? Here, I suggested two institutions. My first recommendation was that people concerned with the plight of the poor in general, and specifically with future unfortunates such as those now victimized by Katrina, donate money to the Mises Institute. In this regard, one of my critics challenged: "How is funding Mises going to influence the disposition of 250,000 homeless unemployed?"

I readily "concede" that this Auburn, Alabama institution will not directly devote itself to the care and feeding of the New Orleans homeless. They are simply not in the business of handing out bottles of water, food and housing accommodations to refugees. But this misconstrues my suggestion. I was urging support of the Mises Institute not as a short run solution, but as a LONG RUN one.

How so? Funding the Mises Institute (and LewRockwell.com) will promote free enterprise. If Bill Gates or George Soros were to give this organization just $1 billion, a mere pittance for people of this sort, the market system will be given a gigantic boost. Not only in the future, when hundreds more Austro-libertarians will become professors, journalists, etc., but even in the immediate future. Just think in terms of a new *Washington Post* with Lew Rockwell as publisher. Or, imagine a new Fox News with Lew as the editor. That's point one.

Point two is that to the degree a country embraces libertarianism and economic freedom, it becomes richer, far richer. (For those of you who are empirically oriented, for an illustration of that claim, see, James Gwartney, Robert Lawson, and Walter Block, *Economic Freedom of the World, 1975–1995*.)

Point three is that with a radically richer society, it would be just that much easier for people in the U.S. to come to the rescue of "250,000 homeless unemployed." And not through welfare checks either, but rather via the creation of new employment to produce still more wealth.

Nor does the Mises Institute and LRC stand merely for free enterprise. They also urge an end to U.S. imperialism abroad (e.g., Iraq and Afghanistan, at present). Bringing back the troops as soon as possible would create still additional wealth, with which to help, further, the "250,000 homeless unemployed."

Moreover, the Mises Institute opposes regulations, such as the minimum wage law and coercive union legislation that are responsible for unemployment. By the way, it is an economic fallacy that additional wealth is needed to give jobs to these "250,000 homeless unemployed." Even if we were half as rich as we now are, everyone could be employed in the absence of government laws that preclude such a situation.

Please realize several things in this regard. First, I am not employed by the Mises Institute and thus cannot speak in their behalf. I am a member of the senior faculty along with a dozen others, but this means only that my advice is sometimes sought, and I am regularly invited to speak at Mises events, but always on a contractual basis. The views expressed above are only my own opinion.

Second, the Mises Institute was not the only organization I advised that people contribute to, in my column on Katrina. I also mention LewRockwell.com, and the Libertarian Parties of Louisiana, Mississippi, and Alabama. They, too, play an important role in raising public appreciation for the free enterprise system in those states, where it is most sorely needed in the aftermath of the hurricane.

What I continue to regard as these eminently reasonable statements on my part were met with a storm of protest. Political parties are evil, including, even the Libertarian Party. Anyone who locates himself in the Belly of the Beast (Washington, D.C.) will soon "grow in office," like Cato, and eschew their prior free enterprise principles. Politics is a creation of the Devil.

Not so, not so. Ron Paul is exhibit "A" for the case to the contrary. And he is only the tip of the iceberg. There are numerous elected Libertarian Party members, all over the country, who have not compromised on their principles by one iota. And, there are plenty of former once very able and accomplished libertarians who have renounced their prior ideology, who have not been connected with politics in any way (Murray Rothbard is presumably spinning in his grave over these incidences of treason; some of them were his chief lieutenants years ago). Yes, there is a tendency to take on left liberal, and neo-con positions when located within the beltway. But this certainly does not apply to all. Even the Mises Institute for a time had an office in Washington D.C., where Lew Rockwell had been Ron Paul's chief of staff. But this did not lead them to temper their free enterprise message in the slightest.

So, I reiterate my earlier claims. The last best hope for society and a civilized order is the freedom philosophy. The promotion of Austro-libertarianism is the dark horse candidate to protect future generations from horrors such as Katrina. This can and will be done two ways. One, directly, by allowing a private enterprise industry devoted to cloud seeding and other such techniques to stop future storms dead in their tracks. Two, indirectly, by making us ever so much more wealthy, so that we will one day have the wherewithal to support such new technology, and better care for those few who still fall victim.

CHAPTER 33

Social Justice;
A Scary Concept*

O
n many university campuses, there is a push on to promote social justice. There are two ways to define "social justice."

First, this concept may be defined substantively. Here, it is typically associated with left wing or socialist analyses, policies, and prescriptions. For example, poverty is caused by unbridled capitalism; the solution is to heavily regulate markets, or ban them outright. Racism and sexism account for the relative plight of racial minorities and women; laws should be passed prohibiting their exercise. Greater reliance on government is required as the solution of all sorts of social problems. The planet is in great danger from environmental despoliation, due to an unjustified reliance on private property rights. Taxes are too low; they should be raised. Charity is an insult to the poor, who must obtain more revenues by right, not condescension. Diversity is the *sine qua non* of the fair society. Discrimination is one of the greatest evils to have ever beset mankind. Use of terminology such as "mankind" is sexist, and constitutes hate speech.

Second, social justice may be seen *not* as a particular viewpoint on such issues, but rather as a concern with studying them with no preconceived notions. In this perspective, no particular stance is taken on issues of poverty, capitalism, socialism, discrimination, government regulation of the economy, free enterprise, environmentalism, taxation, charity, diversity, etc. Rather, the only claim is that such topics are important for a liberal arts

---

*January 26, 2004.

education, and that any institution of higher learning that ignores them does so at peril to its own mission.

So that we may be crystal clear on this distinction, a social justice advocate of the first variety might claim that businesses are per se improper, while one who pursued this undertaking in the second sense would content himself by merely asserting that the status of business is an important one to study.

Should a university dedicate itself to the promotion of social justice? It would be a disaster to do so in the first sense of this term, and it is unnecessary in the second. Let us consider each option in turn.

Should an institution of higher learning demand of its faculty that they support social justice in the substantive left-wing sense, it would at one fell swoop lose all academic credibility. For it would in effect be demanding that its professors espouse socialism. But this is totally incompatible with academic freedom: the right to pursue knowledge with an open mind, and to come to conclusions based on research, empirical evidence, logic, etc., instead of working with blinders, being obligated to arrive only at one point of view on all such issues.

This would mean, for example, in economics, the area with which I am most familiar, to be constrained to conclude that the minimum wage law is the last best hope for the unskilled, and that continually raising it is both just and expeditious; that free trade is pernicious and exploitative. It is more than passing curious that those in the university community who are most heavily addicted to diversity cannot tolerate it when it comes to divergence of opinions, conclusions, public policy prescriptions, etc.

What about promoting social justice in the second sense; not to enforce conclusions on researchers but merely to urge that questions of this sort be studied?

This is either misguided, or unnecessary.

It is misguided in disciplines such as mathematics, physics, chemistry, music, accounting, statistics, etc., since these callings do not typically address issues related to social justice. There is no "just" or "unjust" way to deal with a "T" account, a quadratic equation, or an econometric regression; there are only correct and incorrect ways to go about these enterprises. To ask, let alone to demand, that professors in these fields concern themselves with poverty, economic development, wage gaps, or air pollution is to take them far out of their areas of expertise. It is just as silly as asking a philosopher to teach music, or *vice versa*.

And it is totally unnecessary, particularly in the social sciences but also in the humanities. For if members of these disciplines are not *already* conducting studies on issues germane to social justice (and, of course, to other things as well) then they are simply derelict in their duty. If historians, sociologists, anthropologists, economists, philosophers are ignoring poverty, unemployment, war, environmentalism, etc., no exhortations to the contrary are likely to improve matters.

Colleges and universities therefore ought to cease and desist forthwith from labeling themselves in this manner, and from promoting all extant programs to this end. It is unseemly to foist upon its faculty and students any one point of view on these highly contentious issues. It would be *just* as improper to do so from a free enterprise, limited government private property rights perspective as it is from its present stance in the opposite direction.

Of course, social justice may be defined in yet a third manner: as favoring justice in the "social" arena, as opposed to other venues. Here, all intellectual combatants would favor the promotion of this value; the only difference is that leftists, for example, mean by this some version of egalitarianism, while for libertarians justice consists of the upholding of private property rights. For a college to uphold social justice in this sense would be highly problematic, in that two very different things would be connoted by this phrase.

D. Medical

CHAPTER **34**

Stem Cells:
A Libertarian Compromise?*

With regard to the recent brou-ha-ha about stem cell research, libertarian theory is in a position to offer the combatants in this debate something unique: a compromise, a principled one which does not consist of adding up both positions, somehow dividing by half, and giving each side part of the loaf.

Actually, the debate concerns not only the propriety of using embryos as laboratory animals, but also of government funding for this enterprise. About that, there is no libertarian compromise possible: this is entirely incompatible with our philosophy, and must be rejected out of hand as an illegitimate function of government.

But what about the research itself, privately financed?

To anticipate matters somewhat, I shall — under certain conditions to be specified below — be coming down on the side of those who support the laboratory use of fertilized eggs. Therefore, it behooves me to assume that human life begins not at birth, but at the two celled stage. When the sperm enters the egg, that is it! There is a now a (very young) human being in existence.

I make this assumption for two reasons. One is in order to obviate the charge of creating a straw man argument. Given my conclusion, logical

---

*September 3, 2001.

rigor requires me to make the assumption that *least* helps my case. Two, I happen to believe, independently of this consideration, that this is the only appropriate assumption. With the advent of modern technology, birth is becoming merely a matter of a change of address. Whether the baby lives on the inside of the womb, or in a test tube, or in a host mother, is quickly becoming almost (if not quite) a matter of indifference as far as its health, well-being, and survival is concerned. The real change is not eviction from the placenta, but rather the move from separated sperm and egg, which will not grow into a human being in that state, to one where the sperm enters the egg, which will result in the creation of a new member of our species.

With this as background, we now move on to a consideration of the libertarian theory of child possession. Please have patience with what follows: it will sound at first glance somewhat cavalier, even cruel and cold. But this is because cool dispassionate language is sometimes required to address exceedingly vexing problems.

Youngsters occupy a middle ground, homesteading wise, between ownership of property, such as a cow, and that concerning other people, which does not exist. The way to demonstrate ownership in an hitherto unowned bovine is to domesticate it; once the homesteading period is over, you are the proper and complete owner.

Precisely the same logic applies to the child. The arch-typical way to homestead an infant is to engage in sexual intercourse, and then provide a "home" for it for nine months, and thereafter. But if a male and female scientist inserted a sperm belonging to one of them into an egg belonging to the other, and then grew the resulting embryo in a test tube, or in a willing host mother, and then cared for the baby after the nine month gestation period, they, too, would be considered the proper parents. The only difference between the cow and the child is that in the former case outright ownership is possible, while in the latter all that is "owned" is the right to continue to homestead (e.g., care for) the child. Doing so establishes the right to keep doing so, until the youngster reaches adulthood.

Are there any positive obligations to bring up a child? No, in the libertarian philosophy, there are only the negative requirements that one keep ones mitts off the persons and legitimately owned property of another. If a parent wishes to abandon a baby he has been raising in the past, and notifies the proper authorities (e.g., a church, a hospital, an adoption agency, etc.) he violates no libertarian law. (However, no positive obligations notwithstanding, if he abandons the child without notification, e.g., starves it in his own home, he is guilty of murder. This would be akin to forestalling; refusing to homestead unowned land, but putting a fence around it so that no one else can homestead it either; this would be a violation of the libertarian code. When done to a human child, this rises to the level of a capital crime.)

Suppose a parent wishes to abandon a child, makes this wish publicly known, but finds no one else willing to take on this responsibility. Then and only then may this child be killed. This does indeed sound cruel and heartless, but it is the only way to consistently apply the libertarian stricture against positive obligations. The only time a child can be legitimately consigned to death is if there is no one, absolutely no one in the entire world, willing to take care of it. If a parent wants to stop homesteading his child, e.g., caring for it, then he loses all rights to it; the rights of any other would be adoptive parent supersedes his own, even if he is the "natural" parent. "Use it or lose it," would be the libertarian motto for child abandonment.

There was a case in Canada where a father "mercy" killed his severely handicapped daughter. Under libertarian law, he would be treated as a murderer. His mistake was not first offering his child up for adoption. Were there anyone else willing to care for her, he would not have been entitled to kill her. It is only if no one else were to step forward in this regard that his action would then be considered legitimate.

Now to the compromise position on stem cell research.

Allow all those who wish to do research on embryos to create as many of them as they wish. (To do so is not to contravene the one libertarian legal axiom of non-aggression against non-aggressors). It matters not one whit whether these embryos are unneeded frozen left overs from in vitro fertility clinics, or are created *de novo* for the express purpose of medical research. It is also a matter of complete indifference, as far as libertarian law is concerned, whether the "activated egg" has a sperm cell in it, or a transferred nuclei from a non-somatic area of the body. As long as the egg fertilized in either manner will eventuate in a child when properly housed, it is a human being at that point, by stipulation.

The medical experimenters can treat these fetuses as laboratory animals, as is their desire, contingent on one and only one stipulation: that no one else in the world wishes to raise these very young infants on their own. If there are adoptive parents forthcoming (presumably from the pro-life community, but not at all necessarily limited to it) then their rights trump those of the creators of the fertilized egg, since the latter do not wish to homestead them, e.g., protect them from harm, while the former do. The people who want to homestead (care for and raise) these fetuses get first crack at them. (And this goes for those in the womb too, when, if and to the degree that medical science makes such transfers possible.) It is only if there are no takers that those who wish to use fertilized eggs for research purposes can do so.

If allowed, this scenario will constitute a true compromise between the contending forces on the stem cell research debate. It will be an empirical issue as to which side will win the fertilized egg "race." Will the demand on the part of potential adoptive parents outstrip the supply of fetuses that can be created in the laboratory? If so, then not a single one of them will be killed, and no research will take place. Or, will the ability of the medical technicians to create fetuses in this way overwhelm the willingness of adoptive parents to bring them up? If so, then some fetuses will be saved, those who are adopted, and others will be destroyed in medical research, the ones which exceed the demand of adoptive parents.

But in neither eventuality will the libertarian legal code be contravened. In our presently lawless society, that is not a benefit that should be overlooked.

CHAPTER 35

Dr. Government;
The Bureaucrat With
the Stethoscope*

SOCIALIZED MEDICINE IS THE PROBLEM

Recently, Canadian Prime Minister Jean Chrétien changed his mind about his country's system of socialized medicine. After long and hard opposition, he now favors a two-tier health system, including user fees and private provision. This makes it all the more important to take another look, not just at the surface of state-run medical care, but at its basic principles.

Ever since Vancouver Canuck hockey player Daniel Sedin jumped the healthcare queue with his herniated and ruptured lower back disc, there has been an outbreak of wailing and gnashing of teeth on the part of defenders of socialized medicine. Nor was this the only such high-profile case. About a year ago Grizzlies basketball center Bryant "Big Country" Reeves hurt his ankle and was similarly catapulted to the head of the medical waiting list. But beyond such headline-grabbing cases there are numerous other privileged characters: politicians and bureaucrats and their families and friends with political pull, and doctors, nurses, other healthcare professionals, and those who can rely on them for favors. This is called "professional courtesy."

*December 2001; reprinted from *Ideas for Liberty* (Foundation for Education Education).

Most complaints have focused on the unfairness of a system that allows the privileged to receive medical care within a few days of an injury, while forcing others to wait weeks and even months, if not years. But this is exactly backward. The problem is not that some few people are treated quickly, as they should be. It's that we aren't all dealt with like members of an advanced civilization, where quick service is always the order of the day. We all should be treated like paying customers — and if we were, we would be.

Why are there long waiting lines that do not dissipate quickly? In economic parlance, this comes about because demand is greatly in excess of supply. There is no other reason; that is it: supply's falling short of demand is a necessary and sufficient cause of long and enduring queues.

But to answer in this manner is only to put off the inevitable question: why does demand continue to exceed supply in some markets but not in others? Again, the answer comes straight out of Economics 101: a permanent shortage arises and endures if and only if prices are pegged at below-equilibrium levels and kept there through force of law.

Some people think there is something special about medical care. There is not. Yes, if we do not avail ourselves of it, we will be in dire straits. But no less can be said for food, clothing, shelter, energy, transportation — you name it. And economic law, just as in the case of chemistry or physics, is no respecter of how important an industry is to human well-being; it works just the same in medical services as for paper clips or rubber bands. Impose artificially lower prices in a market — let alone virtually zero prices as in medicine — and you guarantee a shortage.

If any evidence of this phenomenon were needed, it has recently been furnished in three completely separate markets. Rent control pegs rent below market levels; it reduces incentives to supply additional residential rental units and decreases benefits to tenants who economize on space. The energy shortage in California stems entirely from the fact that retail prices are fixed at artificially low levels, thus retarding incentives on the part of customers to decrease their usage, and on the part of potential suppliers to bring more energy to this market.

Last but not least, and most relevant to our present concerns, is the health care market in Canada. Here, too, consumers are prevented by law from paying prices that reflect the scarcity value of medical services. We do this, of course, out of misguided compassion. But this policy is based on blatant economic illiteracy. Canadians think they can violate economic law with impunity. They cannot.

Our much-vaunted (in coercive socialistic circles, that is) health care system is predicated on a violation of economic principles. It is built on a foundation of quicksand.

RESCIND SOCIALIZED MEDICINE

The only way to enable all citizens to enjoy the benefits now accorded only to a Sedin, a Reeves, or other medically privileged characters, is to completely rescind socialized medicine. It should be privatized and take its place among all other industries (cars, computers, chalk) that contribute mightily to our advanced standard of living, with no queues for anyone, thank you. This step would, with one fell swoop, radically reduce waiting lists and the brain-drain of Canadian doctors and nurses as well. Chrétien's recent conversion is too little too late if we want the healthcare system to function as well as these other industries do.

Adam Smith's invisible hand of the market works its magic in every industry known to man. Health care is no exception. Those who take the opposite point of view are responsible for the needless suffering of the sick who cannot get timely help, thanks to medical socialism. This system did not work in the USSR. It cannot function with regard to Canadian health care either. Must we suffer through this for 70 years as the unfortunate Russians did? You don't like queue jumpers? Get used to it. It was part and parcel of the old Soviet system, and there is no way we can escape this if we copy the Soviets in health care.

At this point the critic will retort, "It is not fair to charge people market prices for health care; the rich will be treated better." But that is precisely the point of being richer in the first place. If the wealthy did not get better treatment, what would be the point in trying to amass riches? (And if they didn't try to amass riches, the entire economy would tank, not just health care.) In any case, the better-off are already advantaged under the present system: they can jump queues in Canada or take their business to the United States.

Another obligation: there's nothing for the poor in returning health care to the private sector. Nonsense. The poverty-stricken are treated far better in capitalist countries than anywhere else, and medical service is again no exception. Yes, of course, the impecunious have to wait for the well-off to purchase MRIs (many small states in America have more of them than all of Canada does), but when they do, low-income people too can avail themselves of high-tech diagnostics. This is precisely why the poor have color televisions, computers, cars, and more. Had these too, been socialized, they would still be toys reserved for the rich.

IV.

Libertarian Theory

CHAPTER **36**

Turning Their Coats For the State*

The non-aggression axiom is the lynchpin of the philosophy of libertarianism. It states, simply, that it shall be legal for anyone to do anything he wants, provided only that he not initiate (or threaten) violence against the person or legitimately owned property of another. That is, in the free society, one has the right to manufacture, buy, or sell any good or service at any mutually agreeable terms. Thus, there would be no victimless crime prohibitions, price controls, government regulation of the economy, etc.

If the non-aggression axiom is the basic building block of libertarianism, private property rights based on (Lockean and Rothbardian) homesteading principles are the foundation. For if A reaches into B's pocket, pulls out his wallet and runs away with it, we cannot know that is the aggressor and B the victim. It may be that A is merely repossessing his own wallet, the one B stole from him yesterday. But given a correct grounding in property rights, the non-aggression axiom is a very powerful tool in the war of ideas. For most individuals believe, and fervently so, that it is wrong to invade other people or their property. Who, after all, favors theft, murder or rape? With this as an entering wedge, libertarians are free to apply this axiom to all of human action, including, radically, to unions, taxes, and even government itself.

---

*February 17, 2003.

The non-aggression axiom and private property rights theory which underlies it have recently come under furious attack, amazingly, from commentators actually calling themselves libertarians. Let us consider two cases posed by these people.

First, you are standing on the balcony of a 25-story high-rise apartment when, much to your dismay, you lose your footing and fall out. Happily, in your downward descent, you manage to grab onto a flagpole protruding from the 15th floor of the balcony of another apartment, ten floors below. Unhappily, the owner of this apartment comes out to her balcony, states that you are protesting by holding on to her flag pole, and demands that you let go (e.g., drop another 15 floors to your death). You protest that you only want to hand walk your way down the flag pole, into her apartment, and then right out of it, but she is adamant. As a libertarian, are you bound to obey her?

Second case. You are lost in the woods, freezing, with no food. You will die without shelter and a meal. Fortunately, you come upon a warm cabin stocked with staples. You intend to eat, stay the night, leave your business card, and pay double any reasonable price that could be asked. Unfortunately, the cabin has a sign posted on the door: "Warning. Private Property. No Trespassing." Do you tamely go off into the woods and die?

Opponents of the non-aggression axiom maintain that you have no obligation to die in either of these cases, much less in the name of private property rights. In their view these concepts have been adopted to *promote* human life and well-being, which, ordinarily, they do, and superlatively so. But in these exceptional cases, where the non-aggression standard would be contrary to utilitarian principles, it should be jettisoned. The non-aggression principle, for them, is a good rule of thumb, which sometimes, rarely, should be ignored.

There are several grave problems with these critiques of the non-aggression axiom.

1. They misunderstand the nature of libertarianism. These arguments implicitly assume that libertarianism is a moral philosophy, a guide to proper behavior, as it were. Should the flagpole hanger let go? Should the hiker go off and die? But libertarianism is a theory concerned with the justified use of aggression, or violence, based on property rights, not morality. Therefore, the only proper questions which can be addressed in this philosophy are of the sort, if the flagpole hanger attempts to come in to the apartment, and the occupant shoots him for trespassing, Would the forces of law and order punish the homeowner? Or, if the owner of the cabin in

the woods sets up a booby trap, such that when someone forces his way into his property he gets a face full of buckshot, Would he be guilty of a law violation? When put in this way, the answer is clear. The owner in each case is in the right, and the trespasser in the wrong. If force is used to protect property rights, even deadly force, the owner is not guilty of the violation of any licit law.

2. These examples purposefully try to place us in the mind of the criminal perpetrator of the crime of trespass. We are invited, that is, to empathize with the flag pole hanger, and the hiker, not the respective property owners. But let us reverse this perspective. Suppose the owner of the apartment on the 15th floor has recently been victimized by a rape, perpetrated upon her by a member of the same ethnic or racial group as the person now hand walking his way down her flag pole, soon to uninvitedly enter her apartment. May she not shoot him in self-defense before he enters her premises? Or, suppose that the owner of the cabin in the woods has been victimized by several break-ins in the past few months, and has finally decided to do something in defense of his property. Or, suppose that the owner, himself, views his cabin as his own life preserver. Then, may he not take steps to safeguard his property? To ask these questions is to answer them, at least for the consistent libertarian.

3. The criticisms of libertarian property rights theory base their views on the philosophy of emergencies. The non-aggression axiom is all well and good in ordinary circumstances, but when there are lifeboat situations, all bets are off. The problem, however, with violating libertarian law for special exigencies is that these occurrences are more commonplace than supposed. Right now, there are numerous people dying of starvation in poor parts of the world. Some are suffering from illnesses which could be cured cheaply, e.g., by penicillin. We have all read those advertisements placed by aid agencies: "Here is little Maria. You can save her, and her entire village, by sending us some modest amount of money each month."

In point of fact, many so called libertarians who have attacked the non-aggression axiom on these emergency grounds live in housing of a middle class level or better; drive late model cars; eat well; have jewelry; send their children to pricey colleges. If they truly believed in their critiques, none of this would be true. For if the cabin owner and the apartment dweller are to give up their property rights to save the hiker and the flagpole hanger, then *they* must give up their comfortable middle-class life styles in behalf of all the easily cured sick and starving people in the world. That they have not done so shows they do not even take their own arguments seriously.

The logical implication of their coercive welfarist argument is far worse than merely being required to give a few dollars a month to a relief agency. For suppose they do this. Their standard of living will *still* be far greater than those on the verge of death from straightened circumstances. No, as long as these relatively rich "libertarians" have enough money to keep themselves from dying from poverty, the logic of their argument compels them to give every penny they own over and above that level to alleviate the plight of the endangered poor.

CHAPTER 37

The Libertarian Axiom
and Jonah Goldberg, Neo-Con*

The foundation of libertarianism is the non-aggression axiom. This states that it is illicit to initiate or threaten invasive violence against a man or his legitimately owned property. Murray Rothbard characterized this as "plumb line" libertarianism: follow this one principle, and you will be able to infer the libertarian position on all issues, without exception.

Before considering the latest Jonah Goldberg criticism of this philosophy (saving a friend from suicide by force), consider, perhaps, an even more difficult case.

You are standing in the path of an onrushing boulder, completely unaware of your fate. In a second, this massive rock will hit you, and you will die. (Let us stipulate the truth of this supposition.) Instead, however, I push you out of its path, and into safety. The only trouble is, as a result of it, although I have saved your life, I also broke your arm.

Now, if you are a reasonable sort of person, you will be grateful to me. Instead, you insist upon sticking to the literal letter of libertarian law, and sue me for damages for the injury you have sustained. After all, I did initiate a violent act upon your person, which resulted in an injury to you. If this is not assault and battery, you argue, then nothing is. How shall the libertarian judge rule?

One possibility is to hold me innocent of this charge. This could be done by adding up the two acts, the life-saving and the arm-breaking, and

---

*November 10, 2001.

deciding that the former is far more important than the latter. So much so that the one ought to be in effect "subtracted" from the other, and since the result would be a "positive" (I contributed more to your life by saving it than I cost you through the injury you sustained), I would be let off scott free. The point here is that I committed not two acts, but only one: saving-your-life-and-injuring-you, and that this complex but single act is not one of initiatory aggression.

A difficulty with this line of reasoning is that you might have been standing in the way of the boulder as part of a suicide attempt. You regarded the situation where you are dead far more highly than the one where you are alive, but debilitated. We may assume you wanted to end your life because of bodily malfunctions like a broken arm, and now I have worsened your welfare, not improved it.

Another problem is that these really are two separate acts. It is certainly possible that I could have pushed you out of death's way without breaking your arm. To call it two separate acts is really to fudge: this would only be done in order to achieve the common sense result we all presumably want: to find me innocent of bodily harm.

No, the only proper libertarian judgment is that I am indeed guilty of a battery upon your person. My motives may have been exemplary, but my act, strictly speaking, was in violation of your property rights in yourself. I might well be let off with a light sentence, given the extenuating circumstances, but guilty I am.

With this introduction, I am now ready to consider Jonah Goldberg's attack on libertarianism. Before I do so, let me say one word in his favor: at least he does not muddy the waters by claiming he is a libertarian. No, he flies the banner of conservatism (or Republicanism; despite his claims to the contrary, I don't see much difference), a matter of accuracy and decency on his part. This is in sharp contrast to Milton Friedman, a person who does claim allegiance to this philosophy, and yet uses precisely the same argument as Goldberg in an attempt to undermine the non-aggression axiom.

Consider a drunken A, who is standing at the edge of a bridge, ready to jump. B, a friend of hers, forcibly grabs A, and saves her from suicide. According to our analysis, B is guilty of a battery, and even of a (short bout of) kidnapping, given that B follows up his act of life saving by restraining A from further attempts to harm herself until she sobers up. But now what? Suppose that when she wakes up the next morning, cold stone sober, A still wants to kill herself. According to the logic of the argument of the

Goldbergs (and Milton Friedmans) of the world, *B* may restrain her from so doing for the rest of her life. This is the role accorded Goldberg to the state. After all, if it is justified to use violence against a person to save her life, and this works in the short term, why not for the long run? When life is placed at the core of a political philosophy, not the non-aggression axiom, this all follows from the laws of logic.

Something else is inferable as well. Goldberg is really a paternalist. For drinking alcohol, using addictive drugs, and smoking cigarettes are all slow ways of committing suicide. Riding a motorcycle without a helmet or an automobile without a seat belt, hang gliding, rodeo riding, football playing, boxing, are all ways of risking it. There is a paternalist continuum between Goldberg on the "right" who is willing to utilize initiatory aggression against innocent people for very limited good purposes, and your typical leftist who is willing to do precisely the same thing on a wider scale. It is only the libertarian who stands four square in favor of the non-aggression axiom.

If you really think saving your friend's life is important because the desire for suicide is only temporary, then you ought to be willing to pay a relatively small penalty if this friend then turns around and sues you for battery, or kidnapping. The problem with the Goldberg variation (sorry, I couldn't resist) is that he wants a freebie: to initiate violence against an innocent person with no risk of punishment whatsoever.

Nice try, Mr. Goldberg. But if this is the best you can do, you had better consider renouncing your views, and becoming a libertarian.

CHAPTER 38

Compassionate Conservatism*

President Bush rightly notes that government has been a dismal failure in terms of alleviating poverty. Bureaucrats have thrown (our) money at the problem for most of the last century — at a feverish clip since the 1960s — and the difficulties have worsened, not improved. Our president quite perceptively sees that the faith-based private charities have had a much more salutary impact, not least because they are run on a voluntary basis, and if they fail their funds tend to dry up. This contrasts sharply with the welfare bureaucracy, where continued disasters call forth greater and greater budgets. Jay Leno and his pinko ilk may make fun of Bush's intelligence, but they are miles behind him in their appreciation for private as opposed to public initiatives in this regard.

Why, specifically, have private charities run rings around their public counterparts in terms of easing poverty? This is because the former, not the latter, insist that the poor not remain passive, but rather undertake efforts in their own behalf. Often, they are called upon to personally or by letter thank the specific donors responsible for their upkeep, there being no "welfare rights" in this sector of the economy. When recipients realize that flesh and blood creatures, just like themselves, are the source of their support, they tend less to take it for granted. Then, too, churches and synagogues address the entire problem — spiritual, religious, moral, as well as economic, not just the latter, as does the so called "welfare" department.

From this, the present administration draws the not totally unreasonable conclusion that instead of continuing to allow credentialed social

---

*September 4, 2001.

workers employed by government to throw money at poverty and home-lessness, these funds should be funneled through the private charitable sector. It is a sort of privatization of a public purpose, or a "contracting out," of which many moderate free enterprisers have approved in the past (think tradeable emissions rights, school vouchers, private warehousing of prisoners, etc.). In order to obviate any possible difficulty with church-state overlap, the plan calls for financing of meals and beds only, not prayer books, etc.

There have been howls of outrage launched at this compassionate conservative plan, much of it emanating from those who call themselves libertarian. Their arguments, too, just like Bush's, have a veneer of good sense. They maintain that the key reason for the success of private ventures is their voluntariness; giving the church tax revenues would undermine this. Another difficulty is that "he who pays the piper calls the tune": with government money comes government oversight, and then we are right back to where we started; the private sector institutions will come to resemble their public counterparts, warts and all. For example, the Salvation Army, which accepted some government funding to support its efforts, has just been hit with a 25-page long list of requirements, mandating among many other things that its menus be approved by an American Dietetic Association registrant, and that all its employees pass complaint and grievance procedure courses.

It cannot be denied that there is a modicum of truth, too, in this charge. There is little doubt that anything the state touches it will poison, and private charity is certainly no exception to this general rule.

However, I venture to suggest, this is entirely apart from what should be the *libertarian* concern. We are not directly concerned with curing poverty, or homelessness. To be sure, these come about as a *result* of implementing our program, but they are not to be confused *with* it. Libertarians of course do not *oppose* increasing the wealth of the poor (and of everyone else for that matter) but this is hardly the essence of this philosophy. Very much to the contrary, plumb line libertarianism consists of nothing more than an insistence that *all* interactions take place on a voluntary basis; that *no one* be forced to do anything, except to keep his mitts off of the persons and legitimately owned property of everyone else. (Limited government libertarians, or minarchists, would make an exception for courts, armies and police; but certainly not for the welfare state.)

Let us, then, instead of confusing ourselves with conservatives, remind ourselves of our own philosophy, and use it to analyze George Bush's "compassion." Let us, that is, sit back, relax, and take another look at this plan from a quintessentially libertarian perspective.

We have here a man, President Bush, who is in effect a thief He and his minions have stolen vast amounts of money from an innocent populace (e.g., any taxes at all for anarcho-libertarians, tax funds used for anything other than armies, courts, and police as far as the minarchists are concerned). Libertarians, particularly the "charitable ones" may not so much blame the man as the system. After all, George W. Bush has only been in office for six months; he may any day soon do away with this pernicious practice in its entirety. But here he is, forget about the antecedents for the moment, offering to return to private individuals vast amounts of money that does not properly belong to him in the first place. How are we to greet this move?

I say, in the spirit of that great saint Ragnar Danneskjöld, we ought to rejoice. This removes from this fictional character the responsibility of doing what he did in Rand's novel, *Atlas Shrugged*. There is no need to seize any government money; it is being freely offered!

Now, of course, it would be far better if these funds were directed right back at their rightful owners; very little of it was mulcted from the churches and other charitable organizations. And if the latter turned libertarian over night, they might well take these monies and return them to the long-suffering taxpayers, from whom they were seized. But surely it is better that the churches retain this financing rather than that they remain under the control of those who now illegitimately hold it?

Suppose the Crips, or the Blood, or the Mafia, or the Cosa Nostra, or any other gang suddenly made an announcement: here are several millions of dollars we are giving to the Salvation Army. The Sally Anns might refuse to accept it, on grounds it is dirty money. But why is government money cleaner? If anything, it is more honest in that these gangsters, after robbing us, do not, as Spooner reminds us, have the temerity to stick around and pose as our saviors.

Now, there is obviously no requirement on the part of the Salvation Army to accept these funds. My claim, though, just as it was when the Libertarian Party faced the possibility of accepting "matching funds" from government under election law, that this is a matter of pragmatism, not principle. There is no libertarian principle which precludes the transfer of funds from those who have stolen them, to those who have not (such as the LP, or the SA).

It is not as if President Bush were offering vast sums of money to the "usual suspects" in the business community, who actively aid and abet the power structure in their statist depredations. Neither voluntary charities, nor the Libertarian Party, are part of the ruling class; e.g., those in and out of government who are responsible for our present political economic plight.

Conservative libertarians oppose Bush's program of "Compassionate Conservatism" on the ground that it will not alleviate poverty, and will instead in effect suborn those private charities that have hitherto been part of the solution, not the problem. But it is a direct violation of libertarian principles to oppose the disgorging of government funds to the private sector! We ought to adopt our own unique libertarian voice in analyzing issues of the day, and not fall into lockstep with moderate so-called friends of liberty.

CHAPTER   39

Ideas Rule; For Good or Ill: The Importance of Ideology*

When I was young and foolish (the two don't necessarily go together), I used to believe that rationality, common sense, and pragmatism would overcome ideology. That is, I thought that when push came to shove, and it became clear that our economic or political system was not working, when people were actually dying as a result of it, that it would be jettisoned in favor of something that could actually work, and thus save lives.

1. My first rude awakening from this naïve and complacent view concerned the ideology of socialism-communism. The economic system of the USSR killed millions of people — this is entirely apart from millions more of actual murders also perpetrated in the name of the proletarian revolution — and yet it was allowed to persist for some seven decades. One could, perhaps, dismiss this occurrence on the ground that these people were, after all, foreigners, and the ordinary rules of rational human behavior do not apply to such persons, but for the fact that there were also legions of commie sympathizers cheering them on from the good old U.S. of A., in accents that were as American as apple pie.

2. The second ideology involved the AIDS — Red Cross — blood transfusion episode. In the early days of this debacle not only did not the

---

*June 7, 2002.

Red Cross refuse to accept blood donations from gay men, it even declined to single out their donations for special testing. This would be an insult to the gay community. Yet, such was the prestige of this organization that they were able to stay in business, despite having in this way killed thousands of hemophiliacs, and other recipients of poisoned blood transfusions. (Since then I have resolved never to financially support the Red Cross, even indirectly as when it appears under the umbrella of groups such as the United Way.)

Here, again, was the triumph of ideology over rationality, morality, and common sense. Gays, after all, are "good"; at the very least it is a mortal crime and sin to do anything that has even the slightest chance of insulting these people, and they insult easily. This holds even when actual lives are not only at stake, but, even, had already been lost.

A third episode which impacted my thinking is of recent origin. On 9/11/01, a day that will forever live in infamy, when 19 men, 15 of them Saudi Arabian males between the ages of 25–40, killed about 3,000 innocent civilians. This horrendous event has triggered several further ideologies, each of them still operational.

3. One of the new ideologies is the utter and total evil of racial profiling. Given that these murderers commandeered commercial airplanes, it is only natural that attention would be paid to Saudi Arabian men in their twenties to forties, in an effort to preclude a repetition of this tragedy. Has this been the case? It has not. Instead, while greater efforts have indeed been made to monitor passengers, none of it has focused on this age-gender-ethnic cohort. Indeed, the very opposite has occurred. That is, efforts have been made not only to search other groups too — such as black grandmothers, white children, Orientals — but to *reduce* coverage of the very type of person responsible for the events of 9/11/01.

And why, pray tell, is this? Yet another ideology raises its ugly head. We must never engage in racial (or ethnic or gender) profiling, lest this offend other groups in society, mainly, in this case, young black males, and those who support their "rights" not to be singled out by the police as suspects for criminal behavior. Let us get something clear. The police have never engaged in "racial" profiling against blacks. Had they done so, their attention would have been paid, equally, to black grandparents, toddlers, teen-aged girls, disabled, etc. Instead, they have focused almost totally on male blacks in their teens and twenties. Why? Is this some sort of limited racism? Not at all. Rather, this is precisely the age-sex-race grouping most disproportionately over represented in the crime statistics. Thus, there has been *criminal* profiling, but no racial profiling at all.

And yet, because of ideological sensibilities, we have shown ourselves as a country willing to take on extra risks of a repeat of the World Trade Center catastrophe, merely so as to not be seen as treading on racial toes. For shame.

4. Next, gun control. The perpetrators of 9/11/01 did their evil deed based on the threat of no more than razor sharp box cutters. (There was also the fact that previously, air plane high jackers were not suicidal, so pilots were told to submit in order to save lives). Well, there is one way to obviate future such occurrences: arm, if not all passengers, then at least the pilots and staff. No more crashing into buildings, then, nor the need to shoot down a future hypothetical airliner for this purpose. In any rational world, anxious to avoid a repetition of 9/11, this is exactly what would take place. But ours, alas, is beset by destructive ideologies. Earnest entreaties by pilots' associations to this effect, signed by literally tens of thousands of them, have fallen on deaf Department of Transportation ears. Instead, they have contented themselves with meticulous searches for box cutters, nail clippers and nail files; talk about the Maginot Line.

According to the ideology now prevalent amongst our masters, we are to entrust the landing and takeoff skills of pilots with our very lives, but dare not rely upon them to be armed, even when specifically qualified to do so, as a last line of defense against evil doers. And this despite the best efforts of John Lott and other researchers who have shown that gun legalization saves lives.

5. Now consider Saudi Arabia, from whence emanated most of the terrorists. It is all well and good to seek out and punish the perpetrators of the events of 9/11 in Afghanistan, if that is where they are hiding. But business as usual with Saudi Arabia? Not even a strongly worded diplomatic note of protest? Not only do the monsters hail from that country, but so does Osama bin Laden, the arch-criminal mastermind. Instead, President Bush puts out the welcome mat at his ranch in Texas for the head of this nation.

Why? It is difficult to reject the hypothesis that the U.S. is dependant upon oil from that corner of the globe. But if our purchases of this resource even indirectly enables the financing of terrorism, why do we not seek out alternative energy sources, for example in our own country, e.g., in Alaska?

Let's take the troops out of Saudi Arabia, indeed from the whole region, and stop the foreign aid and other meddling, including the murderous sanctions on Iraq. We can't solve ancient hatreds, but we can follow the example of Switzerland, and mind our own business. Thus we may even avoid further terrorist attacks.

6. The failure to develop oil in Alaska is due to the power of yet another powerful ideology, left-wing environmentalism. It would appear that not only are bald eagles, spotted owls, snail darters, and various types of salamanders and frogs more important than human well-being, but this applies, also, to land itself. Case in point: the pristine nature of the Alaska wilderness, plus, perhaps, inconveniencing a few brothers of ours of field and stream, such as the caribou. Let it be said once and for all, loud and clear, however; private property rights are not the enemy of a clean and safe environment. Indeed, the very opposite is the case. Free-market environmentalism is not an oxymoron. Just go and ask the environmentalists on the other side of the Iron Curtain about how well socialist governments treat the land, air, and water. As long as private property rights include the right to sue trespassers, e.g., perpetrators of mud slides, oil spills, wayward dust particles (air pollution), this system is the last best hope for a sound ecological system.

7. But this does not at all exhaust our tour of pernicious ideologies. What of the much vaunted Immigration and Naturalization Service, which a half year after the tragedy was still granting papers to terrorists who had already committed suicide? Has the INS lost profits and been forced into bankruptcy? It has not. Has this bureaucracy even had its wings clipped administratively? Had its budget cut? Been supplanted by a more efficient government agency, better able to sift through immigration applications, and prevent terrorists from arriving upon our shores? To ask this question is to answer it.

8. And this is to say nothing of the Federal Bureau of Investigation. The failure of the FBI to protect the American public was horrendous. Records are even now coming to light indicating that the lower level operatives of this "intelligence" community had foreknowledge of an impending World Trade Center attack. But the organizational apparatus was so inept no use could be made of this information. Yet the popular, nay, exalted status of the FBI is such that it, too, paid no penalty for its abject failure. Indeed, it is no exaggeration to say that the FBI's reputation remains untarnished in the aftermath of 9/11.

9. Worse, far worse, is the statolatry (worship of government, for the uninitiated) which has taken deep root in our society. For victims of this particular ideology, the government simply can do no wrong. Or, if it can, then the motto of the people is, "My state, right or wrong."

Consider the facts. For years the U.S. government has been poking its snout into hornet's nests the world over. The American state has a standing army, contrary to its own constitution. Nor does it leave these men under arms within its own borders. Much to the contrary, it stations them abroad, in the seas and on the territory of foreign nations. It has more soldiers abroad than the combined numbers of all other countries taken together (and most of them, e.g., from the United Kingdom, are there at the behest of Uncle Sam).

Unhappily, the government of the United States has not adhered to the advice given to it by George Washington, in his "Farewell Address," to avoid entangling alliances. It has spurned the dictum of President Adams to the effect that we wish all other nations their freedom but will fight only for our own.

Finally, finally, a few of the hornets from abroad we have disturbed in their own lands have struck back in a big way. Does the American public blame its government for its unconstitutional meddling into the affairs of others? Not a bit of it. George Bush's approval ratings have shot through the roof. A wave of "patriotism" sweeps the nation. But this is not the patriotism that befits a free country, one that minds it own business, one that limits itself to a defensive posture in world affairs. This is the jingoism of a veritable empire. Let's face it. Were any *other* country to have acted as we have done in world affairs, say, a triumphant Nazi Germany, or a super bellicose China (now *that* is an oxymoron), or a reinvigorated bad old U.S.S.R., the only one with massive numbers of troops stationed abroad, and people in this country would know full well how to accurately label such an entity: as an Empire, not a Republic. According to the famous Peanuts cartoon, "we have met the enemy, and he is us." The U.S. has become the Darth Vader of the earth. It is our country which is now out of control. Yes, the perpetrators of 9/11 were terrorists, in that they targeted innocent civilians. But they were hardly the first to engage is so heinous an act.

Let us hope and pray for a return of the U.S. to sanity on the world stage. But if this is to occur, we must renounce the evil ideologies of socialism, communism, obeisance to homosexuality, opposition to racial profiling, gun control, to the claim that Saudi Arabia is not a "rogue" state, to left-wing environmentalism to the INS, the FBI, and most important, to the notion that the U.S., the first of the modern "rogue" Empires, is really a completely innocent victim of oppression.

According to that old saw, the reason disputes amongst the professoriate in academia are so vicious is that there is so little at stake. But if our analysis is correct, this is about as far from the truth as it is possible to be. For faculty members at universities inculcate their charges with ideology, and there is scarcely anything more important for the future of the human race. Professors are in charge of nothing less than the ideological development of the entire next generation of leaders and scholars.

CHAPTER 40

Sex, Drugs, & Rock 'n' Roll; and Libertarianism*

S usan Lee, a member of the *Wall Street Journal*'s editorial board, has written an interesting essay entitled "Sex, Drugs and Rock 'n' Roll." Her aim is to distinguish libertarians from conservatives. And a good thing, too, say I.

Were this a student essay handed in from a member of my class, I would award it a B-. It shows some familiarity with the concepts involved, but misses many important nuances, and mischaracterizes even some basic points. This is disappointing, in that we would expect better political reporting from such a source.

Let us begin with some of the good points. First and foremost, the choice of subject. For all too many political economic commentators, the *only* distinction worth making is that between liberals and conservatives, or Demopublicans and Republicanocrats. For a high profile periodical such as the *Wall Street Journal* to even have recognized libertarianism as a distinct philosophy is a great virtue.

Second, she starts out strongly: "Libertarianism is simplicity itself. It proceeds from a single, quite beautiful, concept of the primacy of individual liberty that, in turn, infuses notions of free markets, limited government and the importance of property rights." Well put. Indeed, it would be hard to improve upon this description.

---

*August 21, 2004.

But then, we run into problems.

In what is to follow, I offer my critical comments, interspersed with her text. That is, what appears below is her article, in regular print, with my comments in *italics*.

SEX, DRUGS AND ROCK 'N' ROLL
LIBERTARIANS HAVE MORE FUN — AND MAKE MORE SENSE
BY SUSAN LEE

Sometime this month, Congress will vote on whether to ban cloning, human and therapeutic. Conservatives want a total ban, liberals only want to stop human cloning. What's mostly missing from the debate, however, is the libertarian position. And that's a shame. A little bit of libertarian thought would clear the political sinuses.

Libertarianism is simplicity itself. It proceeds from a single, quite beautiful, concept of the primacy of individual liberty that, in turn, infuses notions of free markets, limited government and the importance of property rights.

In terms of public policy, these notions translate into free trade, free immigration, voluntary military service and user fees instead of taxes. Sometimes these policies are argued in a totally unforgiving way so that it's not easy to separate the lunatics from the libertarians. But it's a snap to separate libertarians from conservatives.

"Free trade"? Yes, a thousand times yes. But "free immigration" is a highly contentious issue amongst libertarians. The prestigious Journal of Libertarian Studies *devoted an entire issue to this subject, featuring entries from all sides of this debate. Perhaps the strongest case against open borders can be found in Hans-Hermann Hoppe,* Democracy: The God that Failed: The Economics and Politics of Monarch, Democracy and Natural Order; *Peter Brimelow,* Alien Nation: Common Sense about America's Immigration Disaster. *For the diametric opposite point of view see Walter Block and Gene Callahan. "Is There a Right to Immigration? A Libertarian Perspective."*

While the voluntary military resonates far better with libertarians than a draft, here, too, there are complexities. Suppose that attracting soldiers through market wages, as opposed to drafting them, enables an imperialistic nation to wage war even more effectively. Then, it is hardly clear that the former is to be preferred. (See on this Walter Block, "Against the Volunteer Military.")

And what is the libertarian supposed to make of "and user fees instead of taxes"? Both emanate from a government that, presumably, is operating outside of its proper and very limited functions. Why should the overburdened citizenry be forced to pay user fees to government for such things as parks, roads, tunnels, bridges, libraries, museums, when these are improper roles for the state in the first place? Rather than paying user fees, these amenities should be privatized.

Nor can we overlook "Sometimes these policies are argued in a totally unforgiving way so that it's not easy to separate the lunatics from the libertarians." Who is "unforgiving?" Who are the "lunatics?" One senses that these are libertarians with whom Lee disagrees, but this simply is not good enough. As I tell my students, if you want to criticize someone, fine, do it. Have the courtesy to cite them, and then give reasons against their stance. But this sort of thing is just name-calling; it does not by one iota promote intellectual dialogue.

Reading in between the lines, one discerns that her target is anarcho-capitalists, or libertarian anarchists. These people believe (true confession time: I am one of them) that government which governs best not only governs least, but governs not at all. That the "single, quite beautiful, concept of the primacy of individual liberty" leads logically, and inexorably, to no state at all. In these cases, even the limited tasks assigned by limited government libertarians, or libertarian minarchists, would be taken over by the market. This includes armies for defense against foreign aggressors, police to protect us from domestic malefactors, and courts to determine guilt or innocence.

For starters, although these two groups do clasp hands on the importance of free markets, not all their fingers touch. To conservatives, the free market takes its force only as an economic construct — and even then, this is often reduced to an automatic complaint against high taxes. To libertarians, on the other hand, the model of a free market functions as a template for all things. Not only does the market operate as a continuous process for sorting through competing ideas as well as goods, it also allows each individual to express himself or herself. The latter is simply a consequence of the market's function in testing individual preferences. That some ideas triumph and others fail is necessary.

Our authoress is close here; an A- on this one paragraph. The conservatives' adherence to free market principles is very superficial indeed. I was present at the annual convention of Young Americans for Freedom, held in St. Louis in 1969 (Murray N. Rothbard, "Listen, YAF"). This was the point at which massive numbers of libertarians split from this conservative youth group, and began setting up their own institutions. One highlight of this event was the burning of a draft card by libertarians, which set the young conservatives into a hissy fit. The other was the taunt of the latter against the former: "lazy fairies." For the non-initiated, this was a jibe at laissez faire capitalism.

But perhaps the single distinguishing feature between conservatives and libertarians is that libertarians are concerned with individual rights and responsibilities over government — or community — rights and responsibilities. Consider how conservatives and libertarians divide over cultural issues or social policy. Libertarians are not comfortable with normative questions. They admit to one moral principle from which all preferences follow; that principle is self-ownership — individuals have the right to control their own bodies, in action and speech, as long as they do not infringe on the same rights for others. The only role for government is to help people defend themselves from force or fraud. Libertarians do not concern themselves with questions of "best behavior" in social or cultural matters.

Close, here, but again no cigar. It is not that libertarians are "not comfortable" with normative questions, regarding the morality of certain actions. Rather, it is that they have no view whatsoever on these issues, since theirs is a philosophy which asks but one type of question, and gives but one answer. The question? What is just law? Under what cases is it justified for the institutions of law and order to utilize force against a person? The answer: only when he has first initiated force against another person or his property.

Further, the government is by no means the same thing as the community (the advocates of Public Choice to the contrary notwithstanding), and the group, whatever it is, cannot have any rights or responsibilities. This applies solely to individuals.

Libertarians most certainly do concern themselves with questions of "best behavior" in social or cultural matters. But they do not do this, they cannot do this, qua libertarians. Rather, they, like all other human beings, do this in their role as citizens, individuals, whatever. Similarly, most doctors, chess players and athletes like ice cream. But they express this taste not as practitioners of these callings; rather, they do so as individuals.

By contrast, conservatives are comfortable with normative issues. Conservative thought works within a hierarchical structure for behavior that has, at its top, absolute and enduring values. These values are not the result of the agnostic process of the free market; they are ontologically inherent. Because conservatives assume that there is a recognizable standard of excellence, they deal easily with notions of virtue and moral behavior. For example, they argue that the state of marriage between a man and a woman possesses great virtue. And they can go on to distinguish lesser states of virtue in other types of relationships. This process of distinguishing isn't an entirely epistemological argument, however; it is based, in part, on tradition and, in part, on sociology taken from assumptions about "best behavior."

> *It is not exactly true that "conservatives are comfortable with normative issues," and libertarians are not. Surely, the question of just law is a normative one. Rather, at least insofar as modern conservatism is concerned, their perspective is* defined *in terms of certain positions on what is virtue and moral behavior. Someone who favors homosexual marriage is to that extent not a conservative.*

Libertarians believe that marriage between a man and a woman is just one among other equally permissible relationships; they eschew the question of whether there is inherent virtue in each possible state. The only virtue to be inferred is a grand one — that those involved are freely consenting and thus expressing individual preferences in a free market competition among these states. It is no wonder, then, that the cultural debate between conservatives and libertarians takes place over a great divide. Unlike debates over economic policies, there are no liminal issues. Indeed, there cannot be any because the strictness of the divide is a consequence of opposing matrices. Conservative thought proceeds from absolutes, hierarchies and exclusivity. Libertarian thought promotes relativism and inclusiveness — although, admittedly, this tolerance comes from indifference to moral questions, not from a greater inborn talent to live and let live. Conservatives favor tradition and communitarian solutions, and resort to central authority when it serves their purpose. Libertarians value individual creativity and are invariably against central authority.

> *It is a mistake to believe that "Conservative thought proceeds from absolutes, hierarchies and exclusivity. Libertarian thought promotes relativism and inclusiveness. …" If anything, almost the very opposite is the case. Both are absolute in the sense of having principles, although a sharp distinction must be made between the principles of the two.*

For the libertarian, as we have seen, it is the sanctity of private property rights and the non-aggression axiom. For the conservatives, matters are a bit more complex. There are differences between the old right of classical liberalism, and the Buckley and neo-conservative right. For example, the former was anti-war (isolationists adopting a defensive non-imperialistic posture in international relations) and the latter two favored U.S. interventionism into the affairs of other countries.

Nor does libertarian thought promote relativism and inclusiveness. I can't begin to imagine from what source Lee got the former contention; libertarians are absolute on private property and non-aggression. As to the latter, libertarians certainly would not prohibit by law private owners from excluding from their homes, and, yes, businesses too, any group of people they wish. That is, discriminating on the basis of age, gender, ethnicity, race, sexual preference, would all be legal. Would it be moral? That is a question entirely outside of the realm of this political philosophy.

All this falls to the bottom line in obvious ways. Conservatives are against gay marriage, they are often ambivalent toward immigrants, and patronizing toward women; they view popular culture as mostly decadent and want to censor music, movies, video games and the Internet. They crusade against medical marijuana. For their part, libertarians argue for legalizing drugs; they are in favor of abortion and against the government prohibition of sex practices among consenting adults. They abhor censorship. In the conservative caricature, libertarians believe in sex, drugs and rock 'n' roll — but it is not far from the truth. Unfortunately, these debates are often animated by the fact that conservatives see libertarianism only as the face of what it defends: transgendered persons adopting children, video games of violent sadism and, yes, cloning. Simply put, the shocking and repellent decline of civilization. But for libertarians, these are merely some of the many aspects of a civilization that is advancing through vast and minute experiments. The exercise of freedom trumps the discomforts of novelty.

Libertarians do not favor abortion (pro-choice). Nor are they opposed to it either (pro-life). Rather, and I concede there is some debate on this issue within libertarian circles, they offer a third option, evictionism. Very briefly, the mother is the owner of her body. The unwanted fetus is a trespasser. What obligations does the owner have, when faced with someone sitting in on one's property? To remove him, but in the gentlest manner possible. One hundred years ago, with technology of that era, the only way to remove a fetus was to kill it. So, the libertarian position implies pro-choice then. One hundred years from now, if technology marches on, it will be possible to evict the fetus from the womb without harming it in the least. Then, the libertarian will be a staunch pro-lifer. Right now, matters are more complicated. But the rule is, roughly, if a fetus can live outside the womb, the mother may not kill it. If libertarianism were installed tomorrow, there would be no more partial birth abortions, nor any late in the last trimester. As technology improves, we would move earlier and earlier into the second trimester with this ruling.

It is very far from the truth to say that libertarians believe in sex, drugs and rock 'n' roll. Rather, we believe that these things should be legal, a very different matter. And, if there is anyone who is patronizing toward women, it is not conservatives, it is, instead, left liberals. For they are the ones who espouse "feminism," the basis of which is the premise that women are helpless and exploited. Nothing could be further from the truth. See on this Micheal Levin, Feminism and Freedom.

To push my argument further, libertarian thought, with its fluid cultural matrix, offers a better response to some of the knottiest problems of society. It is, especially when contrasted with the conservative cultural matrix, a postmodern attitude. In fact, it is precisely this postmodernism that enrages conservatives who are uncomfortable with a radical acceptance that, in turn, promotes change and unfamiliarity. Yet no matter how scary (or irritating), libertarian tolerance provides a more efficient mechanism in dealing with those places where economics, politics and culture clash so intimately.

While I of course appreciate this business of "better response to some of the knottiest problems of society," calling libertarian thought, a "fluid cultural matrix" is not so much objectionable, as it is meaningless. Further, Lee must just about be the first person who has ever characterized libertarianism as "postmodern."

Although libertarians tend toward an annoying optimism, no reasonable observer would venture a prediction on the winner of the conservative-libertarian debate. The outcome depends crucially on where societies ultimately fix the locus of coercion between liberty and authority for politics, and between tolerance and conformity for culture. One can imagine, though, how discouraged F.A. Hayek must have felt in 1944 when he sat down to write The Road to Serfdom. Now, few doubt that Hayek has won and that the economic argument has been settled in favor of free markets. What remains is the battle over politics and culture. One down, two to go.

Why are we libertarians "annoyingly optimistic?" This is sophomoric; any student of mine who wrote such bilge would feel my editorial wrath. Dear Miss Lee: If you are going to criticize a political philosophy, any of them, try to be specific.

She is also very much mistaken about Hayek's book. This is hardly the bastion of free markets it is widely thought to be. Rather, it "leaks" all over the place, making compromise after compromise with the socialism of its day (see on this Walter Block, "Hayek's Road to Serfdom").

Were this written by a student of mine, I would have emphasized the positive more than I have done so here. But this is an adult journalist, from whom we readers have a right to expect more, and better. Nevertheless, she did do a reasonably good job, despite all these errors. After all, the usual mainstream journalistic description of libertarianism is to dismiss it as a variant of Nazism. At least this authoress did not sink to that level. I stand by my B- evaluation.

B. Secession

CHAPTER 41

If at First You Don't Secede, Try, Try Again*

The law of free association is a crucially important implication of the rights of private property (in physical material, and in our own bodies). For if we cannot freely associate with others on a mutually voluntary basis, our property rights are to that extent abrogated.

The most serious denigration of property rights in persons and thus in free association is, of course, murder. No one favors such behavior (killing in self-defense is entirely another matter) so this is not at all controversial. Another grave violation of the libertarian code of non-aggression against non-aggressors and their property is slavery (or kidnapping, which is short-term slavery). This, too, is non-debatable.

There are, however, many institutions, actually favored by "respectable" commentators on political economy, which partake of slavery to a greater or lesser extent. All laws against "discrimination" are violations of free association, because they force two parties, one of which who wishes to have nothing to do with the other, to interact despite these desires. When a store owner is forced to sell to customers against his will, and is not free to snub any of them on whatever racial, sexual, religious, etc., basis he chooses, he is to that extent a slave. The difference between such laws and outright slavery is only one of degree: in *each* case, the essence of the

---

*July 9, 2002.

matter is that people are forced to associate with others against their will. Another instance is forced unionism. Our labor legislation forces employers to "bargain fairly" with those they would prefer to avoid entirely.

Perhaps the most important violation of the law of free association, at least on pragmatic grounds, occurs in the political realm. This is crucial, because other infringements, such as affirmative action, union legislation, etc., stem from political sources. If freedom of association in the realm of affirmative action is the right to discriminate, and in the field of labor the right to hire a "scab," then when it comes to the political realm, it is the right to secession.

Those who are not free to secede are in effect (partial) slaves to a king, or to a tyrannous majority under democracy. Nor is secession to be confused with the mere right to emigrate, even when one is allowed to take one's property out of the country. Secession means the right to stay put, on one's own property, and either to shift alliance to another political entity, or to set up shop as a sovereign on one's own account.

Why should the man who wishes to secede from a government have to vacate his land? For surely, even under the philosophy of statists, it was the people who came first. Government, in the minarchist libertarian view, was only instituted by them in order to achieve certain ends, later, after they had come to own their property. That is to say, the state is a creation of the people, not the people a creation of the state. But if a government was once invited in, to provide certain services, then it can also be uninvited, or invited to leave, or expelled. To deny this is to assert that the government was there first, before there were even any people. But how can this be? Government is not a disembodied entity, composed of creatures other than human (although, perhaps, there may be legitimate doubts about this on the part of some); rather, it is comprised of flesh and blood, albeit for the most part evil, people.

Given, then, that secession is a human right, part and parcel of the right to free association, how can we characterize those who oppose this? Who would use force and violence, of all things, in order to compel unwilling participants to join in, or to remain part of, a political entity they wish to have nothing to do with? Why, as would be slave holders, of a sort. Certainly not as libertarians.

Thus, it is nothing short of amazing to find that there are commentators who actually call themselves libertarians and yet oppose the rights of secession. Were these people to remain consistent with this view, they would be logically forced, also, to give their imprimatur to union and anti-discrimination legislation, surely a *reductio ad absurdum*.

One of the grounds upon which so-called libertarians oppose secession, the right to be left alone politically speaking, is that those who wish to secede might be less than fully perfect in various ways. For example, the Confederate states practiced slavery, and this is certainly incompatible with libertarian law.

Let us assume away the awkward historical fact that this "curious institution" was operational in the North, too. After all, we are making a philosophical point, not a historical one. Let us posit, *arguendo*, that the North came to its confrontation with the South with totally clean hands as far as slave holding, or, indeed, any other deviation from libertarian law is concerned (e.g., tariffs, high taxes, etc.). That is, the North is a totally libertarian entity, the South a morally evil one. (I know, I know; I'm only talking here for argument's sake.)

Would that premise be a valid rationale for the North to in effect enslave the south, and thus violate its rights of free association? It would not.

If it was proper for the North to hold the South captive against its will, the implication is that India was not warranted in seceding from England in 1948 since the latter practiced suttee; that African countries were not justified in departing from their European colonial masters since they practiced clitorectemy; that it would not have been permissible for the Jews in 1930s Germany to have left the jurisdiction of the Nazis since they, too, were doubtless imperfect in some way or other.

Let us move from the realm of the macro to that of the micro. If groups of imperfect people are not justified in seceding from groups of perfect people, what about individuals? If we rigorously apply the principle on the basis of which confederate secession was opposed to the individual level, again we run into all sorts of counterintuitive results.

For example, divorce. Under this "logic" no spouse could leave another if the departing one were less than perfect.

In the words of Clyde Wilson: "If the right of secession of one part of a political community is subject to the moral approval of another, then there really is no right of secession." Either you have the right of free association and secession, or you do not.

If secession is always and everywhere justified, what, then, is the proper libertarian response to the existence of suttee, slavery, clitorectomy, etc., in other countries (e.g., in seceding territories)?

Under libertarian free-market anarchism, it would be permissible for a private defense agency to invade private property if a crime is occurring there (if a mistake is made in this regard, libertarian punishment theory, kicks into gear; in this type of society, even the police are not above the law). If *A* is about to murder *B* in *A*'s house, *A* may not properly object when the police kick in his door to forestall this dastardly act. Thus, free market competing defense agencies could have gone into the South to free the slaves, but once this was done, given that there were no other crimes occurring, and that due punishment was meted out to the evil-doers, that would be the end of the matter. There would be no further interaction. The South (or India in the case of suttee) would then be allowed to go its own way.

Under limited government libertarianism, the government of the North would take no steps to rid the sovereign Confederacy of its slavery (or India of its suttee). The purpose of the state in this philosophy is to protect its own citizens. Period. And, on the (historically accurate) assumption that the Confederacy showed no indication of invading the North, but merely wanted to be left alone to its own devices, that would be the end of the matter as far as the northern government was concerned.

However, even under these assumptions individual abolitionists would be perfectly free, and, indeed, justified, in going in to the Confederacy, guns in hand, with the intention of ridding the south of this evil institution of slavery. But if things went poorly for them, they could not then scurry back to the North, tails between their legs, hiding behind their mama's skirts, because that would necessarily bring in the northern government into the fray. It would violate the non-invasion (except in self-defense) provision of limited government libertarianism, or minarchism.

There would be no "reconstruction." There would be no "indivisible" U.S.A. Rather, there would now be two totally separate countries. The U.S.A. and the Confederacy. Again, once slavery was ended, given that there were no other crimes occurring, and that due punishment was meted out to the evil-doers, that would be the end of the matter. On the (historically accurate) assumption that the Confederacy showed no indication of invading the North, but merely wanted to be left alone to its own devices, that would be the end of the matter as far as the northern government was concerned.

CHAPTER 42

Secession and Slavery[*]

rofessor Tibor Machan, in his essay "Lincoln, Secession and Slavery" has taken the position that while secession in and of itself is unobjectionable to the libertarian, it cannot properly be applied to political jurisdictions which practice slavery. For, if secession rights were allowed to slave-owning countries, it would in effect be to justify kidnappers absconding with their victims. He applies this perspective to the United States, circa 1861, and concludes that Abraham Lincoln, for whatever his faults, and Machan concedes they were many and serious, is still "a good American." Why? This is because he was justified in stopping the Confederate (slave) states from seceding, even though, Machan again stipulates, stopping slavery was no part of Lincoln's motivation.

While it cannot be denied that this is an interesting viewpoint, even a refreshing one, in that it has not hitherto been broadly discussed, it cannot be reconciled with libertarian principles.

One argument which might be launched at Machan is that if the South was unjustified in seceding from the North in 1861, given that the South was a slave-holding community at this time, then the same holds for the 13 colonies breaking away from England in 1776, since the latter also engaged in forced labor of human beings. If the Confederate states must be precluded from seceding from the North on the grounds that they would be making-off with kidnap victims, then the same can be said of the United States of American leaving the British yoke. As it is the rare libertarian

---

*June 10, 2002.

who would oppose the American Revolutionary War, this alone might give Machan pause for thought. However, let us take this argument to its logical conclusion, and posit that if the North was morally justified in keeping the South in the fold, even against the will of the latter, then the same applies to the U.K. vs. the U.S. Namely, that *both* breakaways were improper, however much this offends common sense.

A second problem with the Machan thesis is that if the South was unjustified in departing from the North, then, too, it would have been improper for the North to leave the South, and for the same reason. That is, if the Confederate states had slaves in 1861, why then so did the Union, during this epoch. Actually, long before the "Civil War" there was a movement afoot amongst the New England states, fueled by the Abolitionists, to secede from the South, since the latter favored the slave system and they opposed it. This, too, would have had to have been squelched, if Machan's objections to Confederate secession are correct, for even though the proponents of this idea opposed slavery, still, this institution was legal at the time, and there were some actual slaves in this territory.

(A word on nomenclature. What occurred in the U.S. between 1861–1865 was not a Civil War. This phrase is properly reserved for the case wherein each side is contending for rule over that which is claimed by both. In sharp contradistinction, the South in the War of Northern Aggression — or, more radically, the First War of Southern Secession — was attempting to achieve a divorce from the North, not a conquest of it.)

A third difficulty is that the North, also a slave holding territory, comes to its attempt to stop slavery in the South with "unclean hands." That is, it is not for the slave-holding North to ride any moral high horse, in that, as even Machan concedes, it was no part of the intention of Lincoln to end slavery; merely, to preserve the Union. But coercing one section of the country which no longer wishes to be yoked to the other to remain against its will is to violate the law of free association; it is to violate the rights of those in the South who wish to go their own way. This, however, is not a fatal objection; at worst, it shows the North to be hypocrites. The more basic question is, as Machan correctly notes in effect, not whether or not the North acted in a logically consistent manner, but rather whether they acted rightfully.

It might well be that the Nazis were the worst society to have ever besmirched the globe (there are, unfortunately, several strong competitors for this "honor"). Does that imply they could do nothing right? Not at all. Presumably, the Nazi police captured and punished, for example, rapists.

Now it might well be the case, indeed, it is the case, that the Nazis did far worse things than any one rapist. Nevertheless, in that specific case where the Nazis penalized our hypothetical violator of a woman's right to bodily integrity, they acted in an entirely proper manner. So, too, then, could the North act properly in stopping slavery in the South, if indeed they were justified in doing this, despite the fact that they, too, were guilty of this very selfsame crime.

Take another case. Suppose serial murderer, *A*, witnesses serial murderer, *B*, in the process of killing an innocent person, *C*, and *A* kills *B* before *B* can carry out his nefarious deed. (Perhaps *A*'s motive is that wants to be the only serial killer in town.) Was *A* justified in this one act? Yes, indeed, he was, since he saved the life of *C*, and the person he killed, *B*, was himself guilty of (previous) murders.

But this brings us to a more basic question: would a hypothetical North, completely innocent of any slave holding itself, be justified on libertarian grounds, in opposing by force the attempted secession of the South, on the grounds that the latter is a slave owning society? (We are now also asking the question, assume, *arguendo*, that the U.K. did not own slaves in 1776; would they have been warranted in taking on the role they actually did in the Revolutionary War?) Machan argues in the affirmative, I in the negative.

At first blush, my opponent in this debate has a strong case. Suppose the following: a thief breaks into a grocery store, robs it, and then, when he is surrounded by the police, grabs a hostage. Whereupon he makes the following statement: "I hereby secede from your society; since you are all libertarians, you must allow this. Therefore, I am walking out of this store, with my hostage in tow, and none of you have the right to stop me, or to save my victim, based upon your own principles." If this indeed is the position of the South, then the North was completely justified in not only fighting its attempted secession, but in actually winning the war. For, surely, the police need do no such thing as obey the robber-kidnapper in his curious demand.

But a moment's reflection will show a disanalogy between our hypothetical robber, and the South. For the libertarian police could reply, "Sure, we'll allow you to secede; you are now a sovereign country. However, we hereby declare war on you, first, to fulfill our contractual obligation with your hostage, to free him from your unjustified kidnapping, and, second, to punish you for your past robbery as well as this bout of unjustified imprisonment of this victim." The point is, a refusal to allow secession is a violation of the law of free association. Machan is so concerned with ante bellum slavery, he allows this to blind him to the fact that this "curious institution" is merely an aspect of the denigration of the law of free association. Yes, the southerners (and the northerners, too) unjustifiably enslaved black people. But the northerners compounded this rights violation by *also* refusing to allow the southerners the "divorce" they requested, and in so doing perpetrated another form of slavery upon them, namely the slavery implicit in violating secession rights. To repeat: slavery is but the most egregious form of denigration of the rights of free association. But there are other, lesser versions, such as refusal to recognize the natural right of secession.

The analogy between the South and the kidnapper-robber would hold true if and only if every single white resident of this territory was guilty of slave holding, and every single non-white resident was a slave. Then and only then would the North be justified, not in refusing the South secession, but by invading them, to get them to free their slaves. But the North would *still* not be warranted to "save the Union," against the express wishes of the southerners (after they were duly punished).

Another difficulty with the Machan position is that slavery is not the only crime. If the North is entitled to violate the secession rights of the South because the latter committed the crime of slavery, then, too, they are justified in taking this coercive position against them for many other things as well. For example, suppose a southerner stole (or was accused of stealing) a northerner's cow. Then, based on this perspective, the North would again be warranted to stop by force the departure of the South. Such a theory might well be entitled, "Secession in theory, captivity in practice."

We are all sovereign individuals. When anyone else, be he a king, a thug, or a majority, demands anything of us (other than that we respect the libertarian axioms of property and non-aggression), they are imposing upon us; they are invading us, and violating our rights. Secession is a necessary concomitant of liberty.

Machan, in explicitly endorsing secession (as long as there is no slavery), has come a long way out of the wilderness of minarchism he previously occupied, in the direction of anarcho-capitalism. But he must go further. He must recognize that there is no stopping point. If he truly recognizes the law of free association, he is logically compelled to accept, also, laissez faire and secession, as they are its necessary implications.

Based on the Machan insight, whether or not coupled with the heroic assumption that the North was not itself a slave-owning society, this section of the country would have been justified in saying to the South no more than "Free your slaves, and we shall allow you to depart in peace." Did Lincoln say any such thing? He did not. Indeed, he specifically disassociated himself from any such idea. He rather took the very opposite stance. To wit, that the South could go on enslaving blacks until kingdom come for all he cared; his only concern was that the Union not be rent asunder. From all this Machan somehow derives the notion that our sixteenth president was a "good American," indeed, almost a libertarian, forsooth, in that the South should not be allowed to depart while still they held hostages, and that Lincoln stopped them.

C. Punishment Theory

CHAPTER 43

The Death Penalty*

At first glance, the death penalty seems cruel, unusual, horrendous, and uncivilized. It is one thing, the argument goes, for a murderer to bump someone off; this is truly an abomination, since all of human life is precious. However, it is quite another, and far worse, for society as a whole to kill such a person in response, retaliation or revenge, for we, at least, if not the criminal, are supposed to be enlightened. According to the popular bumper sticker: "Why kill people who kill people to show that killing people is wrong?" Then, as a purely pragmatic issue, it costs more to fry an inmate on death row (due mainly to legal costs) than it does to imprison him for life, and such a penalty has little or no disincentive effect in reducing the murder rate.

What the murderer has done, essentially, to his victim is, in effect, steal his life away. If there were but a machine that could transfer the life out of the dead victim and into the live murderer (I am inspired in this fanciful example by Robert Nozick's *Anarchy, State and Utopia*, must reading for all non-libertarians) it would be the paradigm case of justice to force him into this machine, and make him disgorge the life he had stolen. It would be a matter of supreme *in*justice to refuse to do so. Who knows? Maybe in 500 years (if we don't blow ourselves up before that time) such a machine will actually be created. It doesn't matter. By use of this example, we can demonstrate that the murderer's life is forfeit now, for justice is timeless.

---

*November 11, 2003.

If the murderer is not the legitimate owner of his own life in the future, or even hypothetically, he is not now either. The point is, to reply to the bumper sticker mentality of some commentators, it is *not* necessarily wrong to kill people. It is not impermissible in self-defense, nor is it to kill those who no longer have entitlement to their own lives. Let the message go out, loud and clear: if you murder, you give up the right to your own life. (I am assuming arguendo that innocent people are not executed for murder; given the congenital inefficiency of government operation, this is the *only* legitimate reason to oppose the death penalty.)

Of course, we do not have any such machine at present. To whom, then, does the murderer owe his life? Obviously, to the heirs of the victim. If I murder a family man, for example, his widow and children then come to "own" me. They can put me to death, publicly, and charge admission for this event, or they can force me to do hard labor for the rest of my miserable life, the proceeds to go to them. It is a crime and a disgrace that such criminals now enjoy air conditioning, television, exercise rooms, etc. They owe a debt to (the heirs of) their victims, who are now, to add insult to injury, forced to pay again, through taxes, to maintain these miscreants in a relatively luxurious life, compared to what they richly deserve.

As for the pragmatic argument, it is simply silly. Yes, economists who ought to know better have found no statistically significant correlation between reducing the murder rate and being or becoming a death penalty state. But that is only because murderers, like most of the rest of us, pay attention not to dead letter laws, but to actual penalties. (It is fallacious to regard murderers as irrational: very few conduct their business in police stations.) When multiple regressions are run on murder rates, not against death penalty status, but with regard to actual executions, the evidence is consistent with the notion that such punishments reduce these crimes. (Isaac Ehrlich has done yeoman work on this issue.) This is entirely compatible with the economic principle of downward sloping demand: the higher the price, the less people wish to access. This holds for *all* human endeavor: cars, pizza, and, yes, murder too. Nor is it possible not to regard murder as a stiffer penalty than life in prison. Were this not so, we would scarcely find the denizens of death row trying desperately to stave off, or better yet overturn, their executions.

As for the costliness of executions, this is entirely a function of present judicial functioning, which can be changed with the stroke of a pen.

CHAPTER 44

A Silver Lining
in Unjust Executions?*

I. INTRODUCTION

I contend that there is a silver lining in the executions undertaken by the government which DNA testing has later shown were unjust. That is, innocent men were murdered by the state, and here I am, seeing some good — from the point of view of libertarianism — in these horrific occurrences.

Let me be very clear. I do not (NOT!) favor the murder of innocent people. Even less do I do so in the name of libertarianism. I think such acts the very paradigm case of a *violation* of libertarian principles, perhaps the worst sin against the philosophy possible, apart from mass murder of which this is but a necessary part. Yet, I persist in my claim that some good from a libertarian perspective can eventuate from such travesties of justice. To immediately see why, gentle reader, please skip down to section IV below. For those with more patience, I will first establish that the death penalty is compatible with libertarianism in section II and that this punishment may legitimately be imposed even by an illegitimate government, in section III.

II. DEATH PENALTY JUSTIFIED

The essence of libertarianism is the inviolability of the person, and of course of his property too, but that is secondary. E.g., murder is a worse

---

*August 18, 2003.

196 Toward a Libertarian Society

crime than theft. Private property rights of the human person, and the non-aggression axiom, lie at the very core of libertarianism.

But when crimes occur, the emphasis is, properly, not on reforming the criminal, nor yet even on deterring future crime, however important are these tasks, especially the latter. No, the focus is on making the victim whole, insofar as is possible. Not for libertarianism is making the victim pay, once, through the theft, and then a second time through taxes to put the perpetrator into an air-conditioned cell, with three square meals a day, color TV, etc. No, the goal is to force the criminal to compensate the victim. Under libertarianism, jail would be work camps, to keep the miscreants at hard labor, the proceeds of which would be used to pay off the injured party.

This scenario is a reasonable one, even for non-libertarians, when it comes to stolen cars, cash, etc. But what about murder? Here, we must venture into science fiction land, a trail blazed by Robert Nozick in his *Anarchy, State and Utopia*, where he introduced all sorts of weird "machines." Well, here is another one: assume we have a "machine" into which we place two bodies. One of them is that of the dead victim of a murder, the other is that of the live murderer. We flip a switch, and presto!, the life is transferred out of the latter, and into the former. That is, after our "operation," the now resuscitated murder victim walks out of the machine, and the dead body of the murderer is dealt with appropriately.

If we had such a machine, would its use be justified? Under the assumption that it was the guilty party and no one else who was forced to give up his life in this manner, it is the rare person, libertarian or not, who would object. Certainly, no one espousing this philosophy could see this occurrence as anything but a highly just one.

We have just proven that the death penalty is justified. Q.E.D. True, we have no such machine available, and might not for another 5,000 years. But we have proven, by the use of this example, that the murderer's life is forfeit.

III. May the Illicit Government Utilize the Death Penalty?

Suppose there to be an illicit government. (I know, I know, this is unlikely in the extreme. But bear with me.) Would such an institution be justified in imposing the death penalty on the actual murderer (e.g., not an innocent person)? My claim is that it would. In order to convince ourselves of this, consider a few scenarios.

1. *A* steals a radio from *B*. The unjust government (a redundancy if ever there was one) forces *A* to give it back to *B*.

2. *A* steals a life from *B*; that is, *A* murders *B*. The unjust government forces *A* to give this life back to *B* by forcing both the live *A* and the dead *B* into our Nozickean machine. Out walks a live *B*, and out is trundled a dead *A*.

3. There are two equally culpable criminal gangs, the Hoods and Thugs. One day, while the Hoods are about to rape a woman, the Thugs intervene and stop it. The woman goes free.

4. A Soviet policeman saves a drowning man (a non-bourgeois, of course).

5. A Nazi concentration camp guard saves a drowning man (a non-Jew, of course).

The point is, no matter how illicit is the unjust government, no matter how illegitimate are the Hoods, the Thugs, the Nazis, and the Soviets, in this particular one single act they are on the side of the angels. God, presumably, may strike them down at almost any time, but not at the precise moment they are doing these good deeds.

So my answer to the question is Yes, the illegitimate government may indeed execute a murderer who is guilty of that crime.

IV. BENEFITS OF EXECUTING INNOCENT MEN ON DEATH ROW

There has of late been a brou-ha-ha about the execution of innocent death row inmates. Gov. George Ryan of Illinois has gone so far as to call a halt to all executions in that state due to the fact that several inmates have been killed, who have been later proven to be innocent of the charges for which they were executed.

Let us make no mistake about this. No man of good will, certainly not a libertarian, can applaud such an outrage of the elementary aspects of justice. But, is there a silver lining? Is there any good whatsoever that can come about as a result of the trashing of righteousness?

There is, indeed.

Even though the man was innocent of the crime for which he was executed, he might well have been guilty of committing an entirely different murder. Many of those on death row have murdered on numerous occasions, and were only caught, found guilty, and sentenced for, one such crime. Suppose, then, that *A* has murdered victims *B*, *C*, *D*, *E*, … *J*. And, posit, too, that he was erroneously found guilty of, and executed for, only murdering *K*. Now this latter was a vast mistake; even, an unspeakable one. However, under these assumptions, still, justice of a sort has been done. A murderer was executed. True, this penalty was imposed upon him for the murder of *K*, and *A* is entirely innocent of that particular transgression. But he is guilty of murdering *B*, *C*, *D*, and thus richly deserves his fate.

But what of due process? Is this not an entire denigration of this bedrock of our legal system? My response is that due process is only a *means* toward an end, justice; it is not, and is not to be confused with, this goal itself. In the present case we are *stipulating* that at least some of those executed for murders they did not commit were in fact guilty of committing other such vile acts. Thus, we do not need any due process to determine this; we assume it as a fact. If it is *not* the case, of course, then none of these executions can be justified.

Let me, at the very real risk of repetitiveness, state that I do not welcome such occurrences. Criminals should be executed not for the murder of those they have not killed, but for their actual transgressions. However, honesty compels me to acquiesce in the notion that sometimes a sort of justice can occur even when this does not take place; when people innocent of a specific crime are executed for it nonetheless.

D. Politics

CHAPTER 45

Term Limits Make Me Sick; A Hoppean Analysis*

I f I hear just one more time, from a supposed libertarian, about the greatness of term limits, I think I'm going to be sick.

Yes, yes, I know all the arguments. Kick the bums out. Promote political competition. Incumbency confers Soviet style (99 percent) voting majorities. This way, at least, we'll get new thieves.

There is only one problem with this scenario: it runs dab smack into an important insight of Hans Hoppe's book, *Democracy, the God that Failed: The Economics and Politics of Monarchy, Democracy, and Natural Order.*

The main message of this brilliant economist-philosopher is, of course, that the only justified political economic system is what he calls "natural order," or what is commonly characterized in libertarian circles as anarcho-capitalism, or free-market anarchism. And his contribution to this line of reasoning is superb. However, a secondary message emanating from this book is that, given, *arguendo*, that we must have a government, monarchism has several strong, indeed, overwhelming advantages over democracy. (Take that, pinko liberal democrats, neo-conservatives, and all other denizens of the political-economic swamp.)

And why is this you may ask (if you've been Rip Van Winkling it for the past several months)? Simple: a monarch in effect "owns" the kingdom over which he is in charge. As such, he can afford to take a long-run view

---

*July 8, 2002.

of it, and, also, can maximize his "take" by pursuing policies that prove to be of benefit to the economy, or at least do not harm it too quickly. "Why kill the goose that lays the golden eggs," might well be his motto. As king, he will likely be around in the long run, by which time, to mix metaphors, he will be able to reap what he had previously sown. If he has any desires to benefit his progeny, he would prefer to hand over to them a functioning enterprise, rather than one that has been looted for short-term benefit.

In contrast, the democratically elected head thug (sorry, I meant president) has a very different time perspective. Not for him the pursuit of policies that will bear fruit in the long run. He will not be around then to benefit from them. He has only eight years, at most. Nor can he hand over to his children the keys to the treasury. No, in order to maximize his revenues, he has to grab what he can, now, and the devil take the future. His motto might be "make hay while the sun shines," or "let's kill the golden goose, *now*."

What has all this to do with our subject under discussion? Term limits are to ordinary democracy without them what the latter is to monarchy. An alternative way of putting this is that the system furthest removed from monarchy is democracy with term limits. Democracy with no term limits at all occupies a position in between these other two. The ordinary politician (with no term limit) need not take an extremely short-run perspective. He knows, if he can avoid being caught in bed with a dead boy, or, if he is a Republican, with a live girl (the rules are slightly different for Democrats, given the hypocrisy of the feminist movement), he'll be in office for a nice long while. The advantages of incumbency and all that. Why, several thieves (sorry, I meant congressmen) have been in office for *decades*. "In the long run they are all dead," true, but if the long run takes dozens of years, the incentive to loot and run is somewhat attenuated.

However, introduce term limits, and all bets are off. Now, the focus is on making off with as much of the silverware as possible, in the short term specified by the term limit. Take term limits to their logical extension in order to see them for what they are: suppose the term limit was exceedingly short; not eight years, or even eight months. Suppose it was eight weeks, or, even better yet, only eight days. Can you imagine the feeding frenzy such a system would give rise to! Why, there wouldn't even be the pretense of "public good," "making the world safe for democracy," "a chicken in every pot," or any of that other politician babble. It would be a pure race to accumulate riches, with very little pretense.

One implication of this insight: the longer the term limit in term limits, the better. A term limit of hours, days, or months would be an absolute disaster. Many years is better, and decades even more so. A lifetime term limit would not be so bad, as far as these things go. Then, when we arrive at the "term limit" which affords the ability to bequeath to one's children the crown, e.g., full monarchy, we arrive at the other end of the spectrum. The point is, given any government at all, the closer to monarchy the better. The problem with term limits is that they move us in the wrong direction. If anything, we ought to be *expanding* present terms of office.

Although this can only be speculative, the reason many people, even libertarians, have been fooled by the siren song of term limits is that they are still in thrall to the idea that mainstream politicians (I make an exception for Ron Paul and a handful of other libertarian officeholders) are legitimate. If these politicos were seen in a true light, the last thing we would want to do is leash an unending stream of them upon us, with little or no incentive to rein in their natural tendencies to pillage. If have them we must, then let us wish them the longest possible terms of office.

CHAPTER 46

Federalism: Is It Libertarian?*

I s France justified in invading New York City to force the latter to get rid of its rent control legislation? Would it be compatible with libertarianism for California to forcibly prevent the U.S. government from imposing a draft on California citizens? The federal government physically attacks Mississippi in 1950 for its Jim Crow legislation; Mississippi resists. Which side does the libertarian root for? The U.S. (or the state of Louisiana, it matter not which) forces Canada to give up its Sunday shopping restrictions. Several Crips members physically prevent several members of the Bloods gang (or vice versa) from raping an innocent woman. State policemen stop a robbery in progress. A member of the Murder, Inc., on a busman's holiday in the U.S. (or in Mexico), shoots down a member of the armed forces of that country who is in the act of kidnapping an innocent person. Brazil invades the U.S. because of the protective tariffs of the latter. Little Rhode Island (think *The Mouse that Roared*) forces the U.S. government to leave Iraq. How should the libertarian analyze these occurrences?

We take it as non-debatable within libertarian circles at least that the following are improper: rent control, a military draft, Jim Crow legislation, Sunday shopping restrictions, rape, robbery, kidnapping, tariffs, and the U.S. intervention in Iraq. We also take it as non-debatable within (at least anarcho-capitalist) libertarian circles that the following are also illegitimate:

---

*May 25, 2005.

the governments of France, New York City, California, the U.S., Mississippi, Louisiana, Canada, the Crips, the Bloods, state policemen, Murder, Inc. and the governments of Mexico, Brazil, and Rhode Island.

Thus, in *all* these cases there is one illegitimate institution attacking another illegitimate institution. Further, in *all* instances mentioned above if the initiators of the violence, call them all, *A*, succeeds, and *B*, the recipients of it, fail, the world, all other things equal, will be a more libertarian place. That is, there will be less bad things (rent control, a military draft, Jim Crow legislation, Sunday shopping restrictions, rape, robbery, kidnapping, tariffs, and U.S. imperialism) going on.

Thus, libertarians must *favor* all these incursions. It cannot be denied that most if not all of these incursions would be undertaken by groups that are themselves illegitimate. But, let us abstract from this issue, and focus solely on the act itself, and ignore the status of the person or group itself. Thus, we may readily concede that the Bloods and government of Louisiana are both illegitimate institutions. Both engage in robbery on a massive scale (the latter far more than the former). Yet, in the specific instance mentioned above, both are doing good works. The Bloods stop a rape, and the state of Louisiana ends Canadian restrictions on Sunday shopping. If we focus narrowly on these two acts alone, it is difficult to see why the libertarian should oppose them.

On the other hand, and there most certainly is an "other hand" in the matter, the crucial supposition "all other things equal" certainly does *not* hold true. Rather, were all these incursions to take place, this would be a recipe for unjustified violence on a truly monumental scale. This scenario would imply mayhem; chaos on a scale never before even contemplated. Think the U.S. war on Iraq, multiplied, say, one million fold. Were this scenario ever to occur, it might really mean the end of virtually the entire world, with all or almost all of the entire world's population being consumed in the conflagration. We take it that this too is incompatible with libertarianism.

Governments, in particular, are truly vicious organizations. It is bad enough that they continually maul their own citizens. At least let us strive to keep them confined to their own territories. For when each poaches on that of the others, rights violations are multiplied enormously.

So what is going on here? Do we libertarians side with the federalist centralizers, or the anti-federalist de-centralizers? Well, neither or both. The point is, these two groups are speaking past each other. Some are focusing on one crucial element of the situation, their own, and ignoring the insights of the other.

Is France justified in invading New York City and thereby ending its rent control? Well, the government of New York City would seem to have little ground for complaint, and the liberated victims would surely not complain. New York's housing regulation has done all sorts of harm not only to landlords, but also to tenants. This is true in the short run, and if nothing else changes. On the other hand, any such act on the part of the French will inevitably setup a chain reaction leading to horrendous conclusions, even apart from the precedents set up by any such move.

Henry Hazlitt in his *Economics in One Lesson* tells us: "The art of economics consists in looking not merely at the immediate but at the longer effects of any act or policy; it consists in tracing the consequences of that policy not merely for one group but for all groups." No words could be truer of the present case.

In the immediate short run, the federalist centralizers are indeed correct. Saddam was indeed a bad man, and if the U.S. invasion of Iraq could be confined to the one element, with no "collateral damage" and no precedents setup by it, such an act would be undoubtedly libertarian. (Again, we are ignoring, *arguendo*, the fact that the U.S. army is financed in a manner incompatible with libertarianism.) When Brazil assaults the U.S. and forces it to give up its protective tariffs, this, too, promotes freedom, in the short run. Interferences with trade are quintessentially unlibertarian.

But when we take into account the implications of these deeds that are good in the short run and from a narrow perspective, it is difficult to see how they can be reconciled with libertarianism. The anti-federalist decentralizers would have to get the nod from this point of view.

So which is the correct perspective from which to look at these events? The long run or the short run? Unfortunately, economics vouchsafes us no answer to this perplexing question. It is all a matter of time preference, which, as Austrian economics teaches us, is inherently a subjective matter.

Notice, no mention was made, above, of the U.S., or any other constitution. This is because, along with Spooner, we regard this document as of "no authority."

But this is hardly the end of the matter. There is more to be considered, much more.

First, if France invades New York City to stop rent control, as a practically inevitable matter, France would necessarily be killing innocent New

York City civilians too. The French cannot just attack the New York City government. Also, France would necessarily aggress against its own citizens to attack New York City, by taxing and/or conscripting them.

Second, the real question at issue is this: If a dangerous state is already setup, but which claims to derive its authority from a document that grants it powers, but also limits them, then is it useful, from the libertarian point of view, to try to hold them to this document, that is, to try to keep them within the limits even the state admits it is bound by?

We believe it is imminently sensible and libertarian to tell such a government — "Hey, waitasec — you yourself said you are only permitted to do *A*, *B*, and *C*, and that you cannot do *X*, *Y*, and *Z* — and here you are doing *X*, so you had better start playing by your own rules." In other words, the federal government purports to be defined by the Constitution. The Constitution, illicit as it is, as written would not permit it to force one of the states to drop its rent controls (for example). So if we as libertarians advocate that the federal government engage in an unconstitutional action to force New York City to drop its rent controls because that result is a libertarian one, the immediate and accompanying cost is that we are advocating the principle that the feds can disregard the Constitution. That means we are advocating getting rid of one of the few institutional features that as a practical matter does put some limits on the central state.

Think of it like this: you have a dangerous dragon chained to a mountain. You want him to attack a roving gang of bandits, but to do this, you have to unchain him. So you unchain this monster, and he flies up and attacks the bandits, killing a couple of them. But to keep the analogy accurate, only some of the bandits are killed, not all of them, since the state is notoriously inefficient. We would say this is a good thing, for the dragon to have killed some of the bandits.

But is it a good thing to unchain such a beast? The acts are intertwined. *Both* the means, and the ends, of the action *must* be libertarian. The end (killing bandits) is libertarian, but is the means, unleashing a dangerous monster? Likewise with the federal government: the end nullifying New York City's rent control laws, etc., is good, but the means chosen, loosening the restrictions on a monster, is clearly unlibertarian. And here we dovetail back to the point about considering the short run vs. the long run, which is analogous to the choice between means and ends.

Third, libertarians in our view ought to be *honest* and above board. Whatever our views are of what would be a more libertarian system or situation, honesty and integrity calls for us to accurately identify our current system. If it is obviously libertarian for the feds to nullify a New York City rent control law, the honest libertarian would then simply have to say he is glad of the result, glad the Supreme Court did what it did, even though it is not constitutional. It is dishonest in our view to come up with twisted makeweight arguments that the action you prefer just happens to be constitutional. It is just too much of a coincidence that when the centralist libertarians like a result of a given federal action, it just happens to be squared with the Constitution. It would be better to simply admit that the federal action is unconstitutional but then say "so what."

Fourth, while as *wertfrei* economists we might not be able to choose between short- and long-run preference, as humans with values, and as libertarians, we think we can say that it is sensible to give the long run at least some weight. One does not want liberty for fifteen minutes only.

One last thought. If a Constitutional Convention were in session as we speak, and a bunch of uppity Franklins and Madisons were planning a new government, should a libertarian be in favor of the new central state having limited/enumerated powers? Of course, it would be understood that if the new central state has only enumerated powers, in some cases it will be unable to intervene to stop the constituent states from engaging in certain unlibertarian practices. We would definitely favor such a structure — to enumerate the new central state's power and limit it to only those powers. The alternative is for the new central government to have unlimited powers. What libertarian could be in favor of setting up an unlimited government? So we would choose, and be in favor of limiting that government's powers, even if it meant that later on, it would have diminished ability to stop the constituent states from doing bad things.

And this holds true even if, in the future, we would try to get the central government to violate its constitutional limitations for the sake of liberty in a particular situation. The fact that we would adopt a more *ad hoc* or results-oriented approach on a case-by-case basis does not mean we oppose *having* limits as a general principle.

Washington, D.C. stops New York City's rent control, and ends New York state's wine tariffs. Looked at in isolation, this sounds pretty good to libertarian ears. But from a deeper perspective, looking at the long-run implications, such acts are highly problematic.

Thanks, Mr. Libertarian

Whenever anyone mentions "Austrian economics without You Know Who," the cognoscenti know exactly who is meant: Ludwig von Mises, of course. This issue arose late in the last century, during a discussion of the phenomenon of the revival of the Austrian School of economics, when it was feared by some that Mises was too radical, too uncompromising. He had to be jettisoned in favor of moderates, such as, for example, Friedrich A. Hayek if the praxeological school was to make any headway, at least in this inside the beltway perspective.

But what about "Libertarianism without You Know Who?" To whom does this reference apply? To Murray N. Rothbard, of course. There are those, just as in the case of Mises, who maintain that Rothbard, also, was too radical, too uncompromising. If libertarianism is to prosper, he too, must be ignored, in favor of more moderate libertarians, such as for example, Milton Friedman.

The present book is dedicated to the memory of Murray N. Rothbard. It is fitting that this its final chapter would be devoted to him too, since the entire volume stems from what I have learned directly and indirectly from this great man. He was my mentor, my guru, my friend, my confidant; without him, this group of essays could not have been written.

I intend to accomplish this task through the intermediation of seven scholars, also devotees of Murray: Wendy McElroy, Lew Rockwell, Joe T.

Salerno, Gary North, Ron Paul, Justin Raimondo, and Tom Woods. Each of them brilliantly demonstrates the truly gargantuan contributions of Rothbard to liberty and sound economics, and the fact that in some circles at least, he is unable to receive his justified due.

Tom Woods quotes Robert Higgs, yet another magnificent contributor to the "science of liberty,"[1] who states:

> Murray Rothbard's scholarship spanned an enormous range, including philosophy, methodology, economic theory, the history of economic and political thought, economic history, economic policy, law, and contemporary politics. I was well along in my career as an economist specializing in the economic history of the United States when I began to read his work. Once started, I never stopped.[2]

Woods criticizes the way Rothbard has been treated in many quarters, many calling themselves libertarian, and some, in my view, even deserving of such an honorific. In a truly scintillating presentation, Woods demonstrates how Rothbard has been shoved down the proverbial memory hole, how he has been utterly ignored by those who stand on his shoulders. It is one thing to criticize Murray Rothbard, whether from a libertarian or non-libertarian perspective. That is perfectly acceptable. It is even beneficial, for we all learn from such contributions; we get that much closer to the truth of the matter. But to overlook this giant of liberty, and in the name of libertarianism, is unconscionable and unforgiveable. Thank you Tom Woods for setting the record straight. [3]

According to McElroy:

> In forty-five years of scholarship and activism, Rothbard produced over two dozen books and thousands of articles that made sense of the world from a radical individualist perspective. In doing so, it is no exaggeration to say that Rothbard created the modern libertarian movement. Specifically, he refined and fused together:

---

[1] A phrase created by Murray.

[2] Tom Woods, 2013. "Rothbard was a hack." October 25; http://tomwoods.com/blog/rothbard-was-a-hack/

[3] "An evening with Tom Woods," August 8, 2012; https://www.youtube.com/watch?v= l2IF-wEZLx7U

- natural law theory, using a basic Aristotelian or Randian approach;

- the radical civil libertarianism of nineteenth-century individualist-anarchists, especially Lysander Spooner and Benjamin Tucker;

- the free market philosophy of Austrian economists, in particular Ludwig von Mises, into which he incorporated sweeping economic histories; and,

- the foreign policy of the American Old Right — that is, isolationism.[4]

Each of these points is crucial. Before the advent of Rothbard, if a person favored peace, he pretty much had to be a critic of the market, for the free enterprise movement, such as it was, was almost a totally owned subsidiary of the conservative, interventionist warmongers. Virtually all revisionist historians were at best highly critical of laissez-faire capitalism. Combining Aristotelianism, with Mises, with Spooner and Tucker, with peace and non-interventionism was widely seen as some sort of variant of political-economic schizophrenia, for these disparate strands not only did not belong together, they were mortal enemies. Only in the hands of a Murray Rothbard could these disparate strands be woven into something cohesive, forming the modern libertarian movement. And not only did he "fuse together" these strands, but he "refined" them as well, making important and original contributions to all of them. Thank you Wendy McElroy for setting the record straight.

A similar occurrence took place with regard to the explanation for the Austrian revival of the 1970s, for Murray Rothbard is not only Mr. Libertarian, he is also Mr. Austrian. Some commentators attribute this to the awarding of the Nobel prize in economics to Hayek in 1974. Others maintain it was the conference on Austrian economics held in South Royalton, Vermont, also in 1974, that was responsible for triggering this happy occurrence, since it gathered numerous young praxeologists together. But neither of these could have accounted for the Austrian revival. Nobel prizes in economics rarely if ever start or resuscitate forgotten schools of economic thought. And if the fact that there were several dozen young

[4]Wendy McElroy, "Murray N. Rothbard: Mr. Libertarian." May 28, 2008; http://www.wendymcelroy.com/rockwell/mcelroy000706.html

scholars who attended the South Royalton event in 1974 was the trigger for the Austrian revival, how did they come to be there in the first place? From whence did the large group of academics in the early part of their careers spring, if Austrian economics was at that time moribund enough to require resuscitation?

It is Joe Salerno who gave the correct explanation:

> This handful of scattered contributions to Austrian economics forthcoming in the 1950s, however, would have defined the death throes of the school rather than the prelude to its rebirth were it not for the creative genius of Murray Rothbard, which came to fruition in the early 1960s. The revival of Austrian economics as a living scientific movement can be dated from the publication of Rothbard's *Man, Economy, and State* in 1962, a contribution to Austrian economics and to pure economics in general that ranks as one of the most brilliant performances in the history of economic thought. The book was a two-volume treatise of nearly 1,000 pages written in scintillating English that logically deduced the entire corpus of economic theory step by step from the undeniable fact of purposeful human action. It integrated the insights and theorems of dozens of previous Austrian economists from Menger to Mises into a systematic and comprehensive organ on of economic theory.[5]

Salerno continues:

> Rothbard not only advanced but reshaped the praxeological paradigm to such an extent that his name became inextricably linked with the greatest thinkers in Austrian economics: mainline Austrian economics from then on was the economics of Menger, Böhm-Bawerk, Mises, and Rothbard.[6]

As a young attendee at the South Royalton conference (I was 33 in 1974) I can certainly attest to the fact that were it not for the dazzling publications of Rothbard I certainly would not have taken part in this event. And this is true of virtually all other participants, if informal discussions at the time are to be taken into account. Thank you Joe Salerno for setting the record straight.

---

[5]Joseph T. Salerno, "The Rebirth of Austrian Economics — in Light of Austrian Economics," *Quarterly Journal of Austrian Economics* 5, no. 4 (Winter 2002): 116–17; http://www.mises. org/journals/qjae/pdf/qjae5_4_8.pdf

[6]Ibid., p., 117.

Lew Rockwell puts this matter very well when he says:

> Rothbard was the architect of the body of thought known around the world as libertarianism. This radically antistate political philosophy unites free market economics, a no-exception attachment to private property rights, a profound concern for human liberty, and a love of peace, with the conclusion that society should be completely free to develop absent any further interference from the state, which can and should be eliminated.[7]

Thank you Lew Rockwell for setting the record straight by creating the Mises Institute, which as far as I'm concerned, and of course by saying this I mean no criticism of this world class institution, is Murray Rothbard's living room writ large. What better monument to the contribution of Murray N. Rothbard could there be but a living, breathing, life affirming, Mises Institute, dedicated to libertarianism, to Austrian economics, and to world peace? I know that whenever Murray looks down from wherever he is now hanging out, he has a big smile on his face.

I'd like to quote Gary North here:

> This is how the academic game is played at the top, and the Lachmannians know it. They must seek tenure in lower-tier schools. But the money is good, so they play along. They may occasionally mention Mises in their footnotes, but they rarely invoke Mises's original writings in defending their positions. They do not cite him as authoritative. They come with new approaches — approaches that are more methodologically acceptable, or at least aesthetically acceptable, to the Keynesian editors of third-tier academic journals. They either ignore Rothbard or else dismiss him. They do not cite his writings.

> They have this in common: *almost no one has heard of any of them.* Inside Keynesian academia, they are barely known. Inside free market academic economics, which is dominated by Chicago School economists, they may be patted on the head and invited to serve on a panel at an academic conference. They are allowed to say a few words in response to the main speaker at one of the less significant sessions. But they remain invisible to their peers most of the time.

[7]Llewellyn H. Rockwell, *The Left, The Right, and The State* (Auburn, Ala.: Mises Institute, 2008), p. 404.

This annoys them. What annoys them even more is the fact that the Mises Institute and LewRockwell.com are Rothbardian. These two sites are highly ranked on the various website-ranking sites. These sites get enormous traffic. The Austrian School is known to the general public only through Rothbard-influenced sites.[8]

Ron Paul has always credited Rothbard as being an important influence on his thinking. He once wrote:

It would be difficult to exaggerate Professor Murray N. Rothbard's influence on the movement for freedom and free markets. He is the living giant of Austrian economics, and he has led the now-formidable movement ever since the death of his great teacher, Ludwig von Mises, in 1971. We are all indebted to him for the living link he has provided to Mises, upon whose work he has built and expanded. ... *America's Great Depression* was a key book in my conversion to pure free-market, libertarian thinking. The confidence I gained with ammunition supplied by Rothbard encouraged my entry into politics, since I needed the reassurance that my intuitive allegiance to liberty was shared by great thinkers. Rothbard taught me to always keep the distinction between peaceful market activity and State coercion in my mind. It served as a constant guide once I was in office.[9]

Perhaps the person most responsible for clarifying and applauding the path blazed by Murray N. Rothbard is Justin Raimondo, if only because he did so in a full-length biography. Raimondo puts to rest a number of fallacies about Rothbard.[10] Amongst them that "Mr. Libertarian" (Rothbard, that is, of course) had no lasting influence, wasted his time when he left the realm of pure economic theory, abandoned libertarianism, was a leftist, was a paleo-conservative, was a suck up, and much, much more. No, no, no, demonstrates Raimondo, he cleaved to Austro-libertarianism and peace all his life, and made monumental contributions to all of them.

Thank you Justin Raimondo for setting the record straight.

[8]Gary North, "Tenured Austrian Economists vs. Murray Rothbard," March 13, 2013; http://www.garynorth.com/public/10768.cfm

[9]Robert Wenzel, "Murray Rothbard Down the Memory Hole at Campaign for Liberty": http://www.economicpolicyjournal.com/2014/04/murray-rothbard-down-memory-hole-at.html

[10]Justin Raimondo, *An Enemy of the State* (New York: Prometheus, 2000).

Index

Sowell, Thomas, 130
Spooner, Lysander, 168
  No Treason, 44
Sports, 125–27
State. *See* Government
Stossel, John, 99, 100

Taxes, 57, 132
  to fund prisons, 194
Term limits, 128–30, 199–201
  incentive to loot while in office, 129
  incumbent advantage, 200
Terrorists, 59–62, 172–73
  bin Laden, Osama, 172
    Immigration and Naturalization
    Service (INS), 173
Time preference, 128–29, 204

Unemployment, 108–11
Unions, 88–90, 92–97, 99, 101–03,
  105–06, 1110
  Buckley, William F., as a member of
    ACTRA, 100–03
  less prevalent in Hong Kong, Singa-
    pore, Taiwan, 105
  public sector, 90–93, 98–99
  scabs, 94–95, 97–98, 101–03,
    105–06
  Yellow Dog Contract, 104–06
U.S. foreign policy, 12

Violence, 25, 94–97, 99, 101, 159–60,
  162, 165
  Internal Revenue Service (IRS), 95
  threat of, 94–95, 97, 99, 101
Volunteers, 99, 167
Voluntary consent, 46

Voluntary cooperation, 43, 102
  condominium, 43–45

Wages, 88–90, 103, 105, 109
War, 15, 16, 30, 82
  American Revolutionary, 189
  Civil War, 35, 189
  contrary to liberty, 16
  effects of, 11
  health of the state, 16
  in Iraq, 15
  on drugs, 16, 82
  on poverty, Lyndon Johnson's, 58
  trade sanctions as an act of, 21
Wealth, 53, 74
Welfare, 57, 81, 110, 133, 168
Weather
  catastrophes, 69
    Hurricane Katrina,
    Army Corps of Engineers, 73
    New Orleans, Louisiana, 72, 77,
      79–80
  control
    cloud seeding, 144–45
    hail, 145
    hurricane prevention, 78
    Nissan's attempt to prevent hail,
      145
    using dimethyl sulphide (DMS),
      145
  conditions, 86
  socialism, 85
Women, 1113, 120–21, 127, 130–31,
  133
  sports, 130
Woods, Tom, on Rothbard, 208
Workers. *See* Labor
Working conditions, 88, 109

44308965R00124

Made in the USA
Middletown, DE
03 June 2017